D0955657

The Balance of Payments

For Harriet

The Balance of Payments

New Perspectives on Open-Economy Macroeconomics

Mark P. Taylor

Morgan Grenfell Professor of Financial Markets,
City University Business School

EDWARD ELGAR

Published by
Edward Elgar Publishing Limited
Gower House
Croft Road
Aldershot
Hants GU11 3HR
England

Gower Publishing Company
Old Post Road
Brookfield
Vermont 05036
USA

British Library Cataloguing in Publication Data

Taylor, Mark P. *1958–*
    The balance of payments: new perspective on
    open-economy macroeconomics
    1. Balance of payments
    I. Title
    382.1'7

Library of Congress Cataloging-in-Publication Data

Taylor, Mark P., 1958–
        The balance of payments : new perspectives on open-
    economy macroeconomics / Mark P. Taylor.
        p.   cm.
    Includes bibliographical references.
    ISBN 1-85278-026-6 : $57.00 (U.S. : est.)
        1. Balance of payments. 2. Equilibrium (Economics)
    I. Title.
    HG3882.T39   1989
    382'. 17 – dc20

ISBN 1-85278-026-6

Contents

Figures

Preface

The central preoccupation of this monograph is the mechanism by which equilibrium is achieved in the external account of a developed open economy. We shall almost exclusively be concerned with analysis within the framework of a fixed exchange rate regime. Since most of the major industrialized Western economies adopted floating exchange rates during the early 1970s, the analysis can be regarded in some sense as historical — especially the empirical material we shall present. The value of such an analysis lies in being able to examine certain real world processes which might be unidentified in a different regime. Thus, macroeconomists have found it useful to study, for example, the German hyperinflation (e.g. Cagan, 1956) or the interwar labour market (Benjamin and Kochin, 1979; Metcalf, Nickell and Floros, 1982, *inter alios*). Moreover, the growing interest in the European Monetary System, heightened by the approach of the completion of the internal European market in 1992, adds a further justification for analysing fixed rate systems.

A major problem we shall address is the formulation and estimation of an empirical model of the balance of payments, which allows a varying level of international capital mobility, and which is therefore applicable to the period leading up to the breakdown of the Bretton Woods adjustable peg system in the early 1970s. We would argue that the ensuing period has been characterized by a fairly high and constant level of capital mobility. Moreover, under a free float the exchange rate acts as a jump variable in response to, *inter alia*, incipient rather than actual capital flows. These considerations lead us to believe that a feature of the balance of payments adjustment mechanism which we wish to highlight — the level of capital mobility — may be extremely difficult to identify statistically, in this context, for the period since the early

1970s. In any case, we believe that improvement in our understanding of a period of recent economic history is important in its own right.

We begin our analysis, in Chapter 1, with a survey of the history of thought on the balance of payments since the seventeenth century. This is not intended in any sense as an exhaustive survey of everything that has been written on this topic for the last 300 years. Rather, it is the present author's interpretation of the salient points in the intellectual development of open-economy macroeconomics. Our reasons for doing this are two-fold. On the one hand, we believe it is instructive to trace the history of thought on a subject in order to examine recurring themes and to learn from previous generations of economists who have worked in the same area. Those who would reject earlier analyses as crude or naive are left rather in the position of the man who complains that *Hamlet* is full of clichés. T.S. Eliot wrote in 1919: 'Someone said: "The dead writers are remote from us because we *know* so much more than they did." Precisely, and they are that which we know.'

On the other hand, perhaps we are not aware of or do not know them well enough. One thinks of Keynes's dictum concerning the power of economic ideas over practical men of affairs. 'New' ideas often turn out to be old wine in elegant new bottles: one should be careful to distinguish between vintage and vinegar. The monetary approach to the balance of payments (MABP), for example, can be seen to be in many ways a recasting of the classical specie-flow mechanism, although we shall outline important differences (international monetarists have in fact been quick to claim and proud to defend their intellectual lineage — see for example Frenkel, 1976 and Frenkel and Johnson, 1976a). Similarly, the policy prescriptions of the mercantilists were defended by Keynes as conveying an essentially 'practical wisdom which the un-realistic abstractions of Ricardo first forgot and then obliterated' (Keynes, 1936, ch. 23).

Further, Chapter 1 is, we hope, more than a dry narrative of who said what and when. For example, we attempt to explain the shift in emphasis and ideas from the mercantilists to the classicals as reflecting a change in the orientation of moral philosophy — from the selfish world-view of Thomas Hobbes (1651) to the elegant reconciliation of apparently conflicting interests in Adam Smith's *Theory of Moral Sentiments* (1759). We also supply a Kuhnian analysis to explain the flux in ideas in international monetary economics during the inter-war period. It is, of course, commonplace to point to the existence of large-scale and chronic unemployment as the major anomaly in the prevailing orthodoxy which was to bring about the Keynesian revolution, but there were other anomalies more specific to the field of open-economy macroeconomics which had become apparent during the 1920s and 1930s.

The later parts of Chapter 1 constitute a more traditional literature survey. In particular, we look at the development of the MABP, which must be regarded as the dominant balance of payments theory before mainstream analysis shifted to the consideration of floating exchange rates during the 1970s. We characterize the MABP as making two crucial assumptions which are necessary in order to be able to focus analysis primarily on the money market, as MABP advocates typically do. Given that open-economy macroeconomics are essentially about six aggregate markets — goods, labour, domestic bonds, foreign bonds, foreign exchange and money — two (goods and labour) can be eliminated by assuming that the real side of the economy clears continuously, or at least in the 'long run'. The foreign exchange market must clear under a fixed-rate regime by dint of official intervention at the parity, leaving the markets for domestic and foreign bonds and money. The further assumption of perfect capital mobility (which we shall discuss further in Chapter 4) then implies that there is effectively a single aggregate bond market which can then be eliminated from explicit analysis by Walras's Law, leaving the money market. The MABP can thus be seen to rest on two fundamental assumptions: market clearing on the real side and perfect capital mobility in international financial markets. Further analysis of these assumptions and the consequences of their relaxation motivates a large part of the monograph.

Towards the end of Chapter 1 we survey attempts to reconcile monetary and Keynesian approaches to balance of payments adjustment. We characterize these attempts as amounting to little more than embedding the equations of each approach within a simultaneous system and solving out for the appropriate variables. Since, however, a major difference between the two approaches lies in their differing market-clearing assumptions, any synthesis which fails to address these assumptions directly is missing the point. In Chapter 2, we therefore develop two models which tackle the question of market clearing or non-clearing explicitly. These are open-economy models of temporary equilibrium with rationing, in the vein of Dixit, 1978 and Neary, 1980. When tatonnement processes are efficient and markets clear, the models reduce to Walrasian general equilibrium systems and should display properties similar to the monetary approach. In temporary equilibria with rationing, however, we expect rather different results.

The second model of Chapter 2 ('Mark II') introduces an imported intermediate good into the analysis so that we are able to analyse explicitly the effects of an oil price shock on the economy, in contrast to other disequilibrium analyses (e.g. Malinvaud, 1977) which have generally examined such effects by treating an oil shock as formally similar to a discrete technological decay. Even if the market-clearing assumption can be seen as a useful working hypothesis during the 1960s (there was, after all, virtually full employment and very low rates of inflation), we should expect the period from the early 1970s to have been characterized by substantial disequilibrium behaviour.

Thus far, the analysis is purely theoretical. In Chapter 3 we critically examine some of the empirical work which has been adduced in support of the MABP, not through a survey but by deriving and analysing the typical empirical model. (This empirical model is in fact surprisingly standard — for surveys see Magee, 1976 and Kreinin and Officer, 1978 — so that we cannot be accused of setting up a straw man.) We examine two major issues in this chapter. The first concerns the use of Granger-type causality testing to investigate the exogeneity specification of the empirical model. We shall argue that Granger causality testing often amounts to a form of measurement without theory. We shall, therefore, attempt to put some structure on the problem by embedding the model within a plausible simultaneous system and, under a variety of assumptions concerning the dynamics of the system, examine whether Granger non-causality is either a necessary or a sufficient condition for the weak exogeneity of a set of variables in the econometric sense. The second, and potentially more damaging, issue we examine concerns the use of identities in the derivation of the empirical model. We shall, in fact, argue that much of this empirical literature, far from confirming the MABP, is little more than the reproduction of a money stock identity in disguise. In both cases we illustrate our arguments using quarterly data for the UK.

So far the analysis does not escape the injunction of Frenkel and Johnson:

> The man who attempts to apply econometrics he can understand, to a problem he thinks is economically interesting, is generally outnumbered by a factor of at least five by those who will gladly tell him what he has done wrong that makes his conclusions invalid, without feeling obliged to tell him how to do it right, let alone doing it right for him and showing that his method actually leads to wrong answers by comparison with the right method (1976a, p. 12).

A willingness to take up this challenge motivates the material presented in Chapters 4 and 5. In Chapter 4, we develop a simple portfolio balance model of a small open economy, which relaxes the assumption of perfect capital mobility, but nests the monetary approach as a special case. The upshot is an empirical model in which one of the coefficients (the 'offset coefficient') reflects the degree of international capital mobility and which might therefore be expected to change as the level of capital mobility alters. Previous empirical analyses in which estimated coefficients should reflect the level of capital mobility have generally assumed that the level can be treated as fixed over the period of estimation (e.g. Kouri and Porter, 1974). For the period leading up to the breakdown of the adjustable peg system in the early 1970s, this might be seen as an unwarranted assumption.

The post-war period in general, and the 1960s and early

1970s in particular, witnessed a dramatic shift in the level of international capital mobility, for a variety of reasons. In particular, and as we discuss in Chapter 5, the establishment of the Eurodollar and Eurocurrency markets, the burgeoning of international trade and the rise of multinational corporations each had a considerable influence in this respect. In addition, there was also a very marked improvement over this period in the international communications network and information dissemination through international news and financial services agencies and other media. The prevailing level of international capital mobility at the end of the 1970s had not been foreseen at Bretton Woods and was to play a major part in the disruption of the international financial markets and final abandonment of the adjustable peg regime in the early 1970s. Williamson notes:

> By the time that the adjustable peg was abandoned, capital mobility had developed to the point where the Bundesbank could take in well over $1 billion in an hour when the market had come to expect that another parity change was impending (1977, p. 50).

Thus, any empirical analysis of this period must take account of important changes in the level of capital mobility. In the present context, this leads us to consider varying-parameter theoretical and empirical analyses.

Using a variety of statistical and econometric techniques, including maximum likelihood Kalman filtering methods, our simple portfolio balance model is shown to perform well when confronted with data for several major OECD countries, and supplies quite a lot of information about this turbulent period.

A final chapter concludes.

1. A History of Thought on the Balance of Payments

He shewed me a very excellent argument to prove, that our importing lesse than we export, do not impoverish the Kingdom, according to the received opinion; which, though it be a paradox, and that I do not remember the argument, yet methought there was a great deal in what he said (Samuel Pepys, *Memoirs*, 29 February 1663).

INTRODUCTION

International economics is that branch of the discipline which deals with the relationships between distinct economic systems normally identified in the real world with distinct nation states. It may be broadly dichotomized into two areas. The first area, international trade theory, can be seen as an extension of value theory, since its primary concern is with resource allocation and the gains from trade. International monetary economics, as the second branch has become known, may be thought of as an extension of closed-economy macroeconomics, its concern being characterized as the analysis of sets of macro policy targets with respect to external budget constraints. A further subdivision is possible if one wishes to consider both fixed and flexible exchange rate regimes. This chapter will be concerned almost exclusively with international monetary theory developed within the framework of fixed exchange rates, i.e. balance of payments theory.

The idea of an aggregate external budget constraint is encapsulated in the concept of the balance of payments. Since, however, by the conventions of double-entry book-keeping, the balance of payments must always by definition balance, it is necessary to take some subset of the accounts as an indicator of how far constraints are being met; this leads to the distinction between autonomous and accommodating flows. Another problem is that the constraint may not be strictly met in every period — countries may be in 'deficit' or 'surplus'. In what sense then can the constraint be binding? Just like individual households, economies can insert an extra degree of freedom into their current-period financial decisions by borrowing or lending against a future period: the problem is intertemporal. Two points can be made in this connection. The first is that homely maxims such as 'good households balance their books' have spilled over into traditional economic policy, so that analysis has been channelled into correcting one-period imbalances. The second is that the economist's traditional tool in this area, as in much of economics, has been comparative statics rather than intertemporal dynamics. Thus, as we shall see, the literature has traditionally tended to focus on the current account or balance of trade in any one period as a measure of imbalance and, as Krueger notes, has addressed the following question:

> . . . given any situation in which *ex ante* receipts must be increased relative to *ex ante* payments, what are the alternative mechanisms by which this can be accomplished? (Krueger, 1969).

PRE-KEYNESIAN THEORY

Prior to the 1930s, most questions in the field of international monetary economics were considered as having been settled with a decisiveness unusual even for a discipline which had hitherto displayed an unusual degree of self-confidence. The framework of analysis had been forged mainly by British economists in the eighteenth and nineteenth centuries and was still wearing well without the apparent need for overhaul. But this framework itself had evolved from an earlier system of thought regarding the international monetary mechanism: mercantilism.

Mercantilism

'Mercantile' was the term applied originally by Adam Smith (1776, IV) to a heterogeneous group of pamphleteers active between the late fifteenth and early eighteenth centuries. More generally, Viner has defined 'mercantilist' as applying to '. . . the doctrine and practices of nation states in [this] period . . . with respect to the appropriate regulation of economic relations' (Viner, 1968). That this term implies a more consistent and self-contained school of thought than was actually the case is certain. Unlike, for example, the physiocrats, the mercantilists never presented a common front and definite school of opinion. Nevertheless, as an indicator of the central tendency of the content of the literature in question, the term is useful, although that content has an undoubtedly high variance.

The dominant strands of thought that together make up the mercantilist outlook are well known: the idea of treasure and bullion as the essence of wealth (an idea inherited from an earlier school — the bullionists, see Seligman, 1930), encouragement of exports, particularly labour-intensive ones, and the idea of international trade as a zero-sum game and so of the general mutual antagonism of nation states. Other important themes were protectionism, an emphasis on population growth and hence low-level wages, a stress on the relationship between economics and power politics and the idea of supremacy of the State over the individual. But the core of the system, for which it is chiefly remembered, is the so-called balance of trade doctrine: the idea that a surplus on the balance of trade is a measure of the nation's welfare and the consequent advocacy of running a permanent balance of trade surplus.

A major problem in assessing the contribution of this literature is the absence of anything approximating to a disciplined approach to the subject. This is essentially pre-analytic economics put forward by practical men of affairs. As a result, we often find terms inconsistently used (often by the same author), arguments rambling in and out and on and off the subject and the copious propagation of fallacies and paradoxes. Nevertheless, Schumpeter has praised this work

for introducing one of the first analytic tools into the field —
the idea of the balance of trade:

> . . . The balance of trade is not a concrete thing like a price or a load
> of merchandise. It does not obtrude upon untrained eyes. A definite
> analytic effort is required to visualise it and to perceive its relation
> to other economic phenomena, however insignificant that effort
> may be (Schumpeter, 1954, p. 352).

The dominant idea that a positive balance of trade is an index
of national welfare is summed up in the title of Thomas
Mun's pamphlet: 'England's Treasure by Forraign Trade, or
the Ballance of our Forraign Trade is the Rule of our
Treasure' (Mun, 1664). And again:

> The ordinary means therefore to encrease our wealth and treasure is
> by Forraign Trade, wherein wee must ever observ this rule; to sell
> more to strangers yearly than wee consume of theirs in value (1664,
> ch. 2).

Exactly why a balance of trade surplus should be beneficial
to the nation has been a source of discussion ever since. The
point is that if an inflow of specie concomitant to a trade
surplus is not spent in a subsequent period (since the idea is
to run a *permanent* surplus) then the only effect will be to
increase the money supply. One possibility is that these
writers falsely equated money with capital and a favourable
balance of trade with the annual balance of income over consumption by incorrectly drawing an analogy between the
economics of the individual and of the whole economy (what
was later called the anthropomorphic view of economics —
see Kaldor, 1983, McCloskey, 1983). This was Smith's line
of attack. Some of the best mercantilist writers, Smith
conceded,

> . . . do set out with observing, that the wealth of a country consists,
> not in gold and silver only, but in its lands, houses, and consumable
> goods of all different kinds; in the course of their reasonings, how-
> ever, the lands, houses, and consumable goods seem to slip out of
> their memory, and the strain of the argument frequently supposes
> that all wealth consists in gold and silver (Smith, 1776).

Now, it is true that some writers concentrate on the accumulation of specie as a store of wealth *per se* without reference to the level of consumption or production; or when production is mentioned, it is with reference to the contribution it could make to the further acquisition and retention of treasure. Others, however, saw the acquisition of specie not as an end in itself but as a means to increase the money supply and hence production and employment, stressing the importance of circulation of the surplus rather than mere hoarding. Evidence of this line of thought can be found, for example, in the work of Petty (1662) and later Law (1705). There are essentially two related points being made here. The first is that an increase in the money supply increases general liquidity in the form of working capital or merchant capital and hence is conducive to an increase in economic activity. In terms of the quantity equation, these authors are stressing the relationship between money and output rather than money and prices. A second, closely related point is the increase in the general availability of credit, decline in interest rates and further spur to activity. This is the strand of thought that Keynes picked up in his apologia of the school:

> . . . as a contribution to statecraft which is concerned with the economic system as a whole and with securing the optimum employment of the system's entire resources, the methods of the early pioneers of economic thinking in the early sixteenth and seventeenth centuries may have attained to fragments of practical wisdom which the unrealistic abstractions of Ricardo first forgot and then obliterated (Keynes, 1936, ch. 23).

Locke (1691), opposing Petty's advocacy of a maximum rate of interest, had discussed the inverse relationship between the quantity of money and the rate of interest. Thus:

> Mercantilists were conscious that their policy, as Professor Heckscher puts it, 'killed two birds with one stone'. 'On the one hand the country was rid of an unwelcome surplus of goods, which was believed to result in unemployment, while on the other the total stock of money in the country was increased', with the resulting advantages of a fall in the rate of interest (Keynes, 1936, quoting from Heckscher, 1931).

Now, according to Keynes, 'The weakness of the inducement to invest has been at all times the key to the economic problem' (ibid.), and so he argues that the policy prescriptions of the mercantilists were correct insofar as an inflow of specie would depress the interest rate and stimulate investment. Since the economic problem in Keynes's era, as he perceived it, was too large a capital stock relative to labour, so that the marginal efficiency of investment was below the market rate of interest, a fall in the interest rate would give the required fillip to the economic system; and this could be achieved by allowing the money supply to drift upwards. In Hicksian terms (Hicks, 1937) the initial impact of a balance of trade surplus will be a rightward shift of the IS curve, as the injection drives up both income and interest rates. But as the surplus is maintained indefinitely, the inflow of specie in each period causes the LM curve to drift to the right, i.e. there is downward pressure on interest rates and a consequent movement along the IS curve down to the right (Figure 1.1). As long as the new level of real income (y') is below full-employment level, qualitative results will be unaffected by the upward pressure on prices (hence the stress on the relationship between money and output holding prices (and velocity) constant).

For the classical economists, the implicit acceptance of Say's Law meant that the economy was always at full employment, so that all nominal variables in the system would increase in proportion commensurate with the increase in the money stock on top of the demand-induced inflationary effects. Thus, the impact of both the exogenous increase in aggregate demand and the induced increase in the money supply would be to raise both the price level and nominal interest rates, with the (full-employment) level of income remaining constant throughout and the balance of trade falling to zero as domestic prices rise.

Thus, Keynes rejects Say's Law and looks for support in the literature of a period before it was propagated. This analysis is flawed, however.

As we have pointed out, the problem in the 1930s, as Keynes saw it, was too large a capital–labour ratio, moreover, '. . . there has been a chronic tendency throughout human

Figure 1.1   The Keynes–Hicks interpretation
of mercantilism

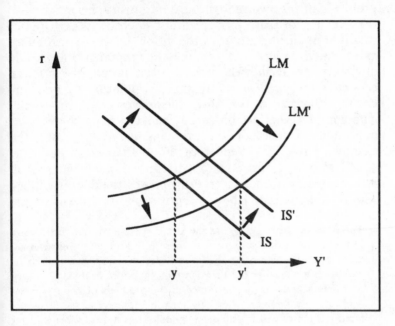

history for the propensity to save to be stronger than the inducement to invest' (Keynes, 1936), so that the flow of investment would be too little to mop up the flow of savings that would be forthcoming at a full-employment level of income. In the era of the mercantilist writers, by way of contrast, the problem was a paucity of fixed capital relative to labour — a low technical and organic composition of capital; the problem was that there was too little thrift, not too much. In such a case it seems probable that an increase in the money supply would lead to an increase in prices rather than economic activity, as the classicals maintained. As Heckscher notes:

> So far from being a 'general' theory, Keynes' theory is appropriate to a situation which could scarcely exist in the absence of fixed capital investment on a large scale . . . (1955, II, p. 356).

Nevertheless, despite Keynes's rather cavalier treatment of the history of economic thought and penchant to generalize problems of his own time throughout history, his insight into the 'element of truth in mercantilist doctrine' is perhaps not totally misguided. Insofar as the inflow of specie introduced extra liquidity into the economy, entrepreneurship would obviously be facilitated. As we have noted, the classical economists sought to refute this by pointing to price increases. But the mercantilists themselves were not totally ignorant of the effect on prices, and for some this was an important element of the stimulus to trade — see, for example, Law, 1705; Venderlint, 1734; and George Berkeley, 1737. Moreover, for Marx's interpretation of the school, price increases formed an essential part of the doctrine, along with the emphasis on labour-intensive exports and low wages:

> The basis of their theory was the idea that labour is only productive in those branches of production whose products, when sent abroad, bring back more money than they have cost (or than had to be exported in exchange for them); which therefore enabled a country to participate to a greater degree in the products of newly-opened gold and silver mines. They saw that in these countries there was rapid growth of wealth and of the middle class. What in fact was this source of influence exerted by gold? Wages did not rise in proportion to the prices of commodities; that is, wages fell, and because of this relative surplus labour increased and the rate of profit rose — not because the labourer had become more productive but because the absolute wage (that is to say, the quantity of means of existence which the labourer received) was forced down — in a word because the position of the workers grew worse (Marx, 1963, p. 154).

In other words surplus value is expanded by cheapening the real cost of labour-power and so the rate of exploitation is raised,

> . . . and it was this, though they were only dimly aware of it, which led the mercantilists to declare that labour employed in such branches of production was alone productive (ibid.).

The real source of Marx's discontent with mercantilism was, however, due to its corollary that value can be created in (international) exchange.

Whilst many economists would disagree with Marx's interpretation, his basic insight into mercantilist ideology is not totally unfounded. Mercantilism was a general social *Weltanschauung* as well as economic doctrine. It advocated the supremacy of the State over its individual constituents, it championed the role of State regulation and institutions such as the various merchant societies and the East India Company. The mercantilist view of a static economic order had its corollary in the idea of international trade as a zero-sum game (of which view Colbert was the notable exponent) which paved the way for the commercial wars of the seventeenth and eighteenth centuries and left the British navigation system and the colonial system as its legacy. In brief, the view was of the mutual political (and hence economic) antagonism of states and of the desire for power; and it was the ratio of power rather than the terms of the ratio which mattered.

All this, of course, was morally repugnant to the children of the Enlightenment, the classical economists; and it was really an ideological shift rather than the discovery of new facts which led to the rise of *laissez-faire*.

It is sometimes asserted that Hume's essay 'On the Balance of Trade' (1752), with its clear exposition of the specie-flow mechanism, rang the death knell of mercantilism; but the doctrine was in its decadence well before this time. It is true that the specie-flow mechanism constituted a refutation of mercantilist doctrine, but like many intellectual revolutions the shift was gradual (see Kuhn, 1970).

The idea of a specie-flow mechanism may be seen as a logically consistent integration of three basic elements:

(i)   The recognition that trade deficits/surpluses are paid in specie.
(ii) The idea of a causal connection between the money supply and the level of prices.
(iii) The idea that exports and imports are both functions of, *inter alia*, relative international prices.

Now (i) was itself an important element of mercantilism, of course, and we have already pointed out that various

mercantilists (e.g. Locke) held a quantity theory of money
(i.e. proposition (ii)) in varying degrees. It only therefore
required the addition of (iii) and the integration of all
three elements to point up the logical inconsistency in
mercantilism.

Locke (1691) comes very close to the idea of an international distribution of specie and even performs the
Humean experiment of imagining the overnight disappear-
ance of half of the English money stock. This, however, is
really nothing more than a crude quantity theory; step (iii)
is still missing and Locke remains a mercantilist.

Again, North (1691) approaches the formulation of an
autonomous and self-regulating mechanism which provides
the economy with the 'determinate sum of specific money'
required for carrying on the trade of the nation, but stops
short of relating this to an international price mechanism
and speaks instead of money being minted or melted down.

In 1720 Gervaise advanced the proposition that 'the
grand real measure or denominator of the real value of all
things' (i.e. gold) tends to be distributed internationally
according to population, since only labour (-power) can
attract specie:

> When a nation has attracted a greater proportion of the grand
> denominator of the world than its proper share, and the cause of
> that attraction ceases, that nation cannot retain the overplus of its
> proper proportion of the grand denominator . . . (Gervaise, 1720,
> p. 5).

Other works could be cited, but it has been demonstrated
that the basic elements of the specie-flow mechanism had
been discussed with varying degrees of clarity, before Hume.
It was, however, Hume's genius to rationalize all these
elements together in a consistent theory.

The Road to *Laissez-faire*: Hobbes to Smith

The twin pillars of mercantilism, then, were the balance of
trade doctrine and the idea of the zero-sum nature of
economic relations. To the classical economists, who

discovered in particular the specie-flow mechanism and the law of comparative costs, and in general the overall harmony of apparently conflicting economic interests, this seemed like error compounded upon error. If the mercantilist era was marked by the idea of State supremacy, the rise of *laissez-faire* saw the apotheosis of the individual, at least in an atomistic sense. Again, however, this ideological shift was the end process of a barely perceptible flux rather than a sudden break, and an attempt here is made to chart only the landmarks of this development.

Smith's importance in the development of modern economic ideas springs essentially from his moral philosophy as expounded in *The Theory of Moral Sentiments* (1759) and applied in the *Wealth of Nations* (1776). Nevertheless, his ideas can be seen as the last stages in a more general eighteenth-century reaction to Hobbes's selfish system. Hobbes (1651) expressed the basically malevolent nature of man's character and pointed to it as a potential source of conflict between all men ('*bellum omnium contra omnes*'). So for him, selfishness was the basis of all human activity and the corollary was that society is impossible without coercive State intervention; each man must enter into a social contract with every other man to give up his individual rights in order to obtain security from the State. Thus the 'great Leviathan' or 'common-wealth' is formed. Hence, political organization is not simply concerned with the organization of a society that has emerged from the natural and spontaneous tendency of man to build up a web of stable reciprocal relationships; it is rather the means that men, driven by fear, must employ to counteract the natural tendency towards dispersion; it is in fact the prerequisite or *sine qua non* of social, and hence economic, life.

Locke (1690) was among the first to react to Hobbes's pessimistic world-view by asserting man's essential goodness. For Locke, societal conflicts arise not because of man's intrinsic malevolence but from the natural scarcity of economic resources: since not everyone can acquire property as the fruits of their labour, some will attempt to expropriate the property of others. Hence, although society is based upon the naturally social and cooperative nature of men, it is constantly threatened by pressures arising from the parsimony of Nature. Thus, for Locke, the State is not the prerequisite of society, but a guarantor of its permanence as an organ that, *inter alia*, protects property by force of law. State authority does not, as Hobbes thought, imply an alienation of individual liberty, but is rather the instrument through which liberty can be fully defined and protected from any attack or emergence of disorder.

However, the argument for the original rise of society in Locke is given to rationality, a law of reason: against the irrationalism of Hobbes's natural state of strife and discord Locke puts forward the concept of a rational law which at times he traces back to the Deity. But when, according to Locke's empiricist method, the origin of cognition is in sensible experience, this kind of approach is inadmissible. There is thus a dichotomy in Locke's work between a rationalistic approach, and an empirical approach that comes to dominate the development of his ideas, but which is nevertheless contradictory to his original premise.

Hume's (1751) attempt to solve this problem was tantamount to embracing the 'moral sense theory' of Hutcheson (Smith's teacher), according to which there naturally exists in man's psyche a 'sentiment' that, as opposed to selfishness, is associated with a desire to do good, in the sense of affording utility to others and being conducive to social harmony. In fact, Hume did not so much solve the problem as dissolve it into psychology; the development of Hume's system is still impossible unless one goes outside his empiricism, primarily because a methodological framework based on psychological sense impression is inadequate for an analysis of fundamental moral concepts — as Kant was to point out (Kant, 1790).

All this set the stage for Smith. For him, the dual nature of man, the coexistence of self-interest and fellow feeling, was not a stumbling block but in fact the Archimedean point upon which to base his whole system. Smith crystallizes the dichotomy in British psychological ethics and at the same time in a sense resolves it, by separating human activity into two spheres: a moral sphere in which societal utility is derived from the exercise of 'sympathy' and an economic sphere in which utility is consequent upon individual self-interest. This makes it possible to avoid the conflict between selfishness and humanity. The main point of Smith's thesis is that selfishness need not be a disruptive element in society but can instead be conducive to order and development, so long as certain prerequisites are satisfied. Sufficient (and perhaps necessary) conditions are that one man's pursuit of gain does not hinder another's; hence the call for *laissez-faire* and the sweeping away of institutional impediments.

This shift in moral philosophy had a profound influence on economists' perceptions of the functioning of society and hence the economy. From the selfish and internecine world of Hobbes and the mercantilists, analysis gradually turned to the naturally harmonious systems of the classical economists.

The Specie-Flow Mechanism

Despite Smith's trenchant attack on the 'mercantile system', he does not mention the specie-flow mechanism in the *Wealth of Nations*, although there is evidence to suggest that he referred to it in his *Glasgow Lectures* (1896). As we have noted, it was Hume (1752) who published the first clear, systematic account of the mechanism, although Cantillon (1755) also discussed something similar. Hume's exposition is admirably clear. The assumption of Say's Law of markets and the impossibility of a general glut is grafted on to the inherited notions of the quantity theory to forge a definite causal connection between the money supply and the level of prices. Little more than an intuitive notion of the laws of supply and demand are then needed to derive the 'Automatic Mechanism': a trade imbalance (e.g. surplus) leads to a change in the money supply (inflow of specie) and hence in relative prices (home/export prices rise absolutely, foreign/import prices decline relatively) which automatically leads to a correction of the imbalance — the system exhibits homeostasis. As an intellectual experiment, Hume imagines four-fifths of the English money stock to be wiped out overnight. Implicitly accepting Say's Law, he posits that all nominal variables decline in the same proportion:

What nation could then dispute with us in any foreign market, or pretend to navigate or to sell manufactures at the same price, which to us would afford sufficient profit? In how little time, therefore, must this bring back the money which we had lost, and raise us to the level of all the neighbouring nations? Where, after we have arrived, we immediately lose the advantage of the cheapness of labour and commodities; and farther flowing in of money is stopped . . . (Hume, 1752).

Further, money is attracted in proportion to the 'degree of industry' in the economy, so that countries with, for example, a more productive labour force will be able to sustain a higher level of money stock. An analogy is drawn between an international economic system and a system of hydraulics, where the capaciousness of any particular vessel represents the 'degree of industry' of an economy:

All water, wherever it communicates, remains always at a level. Ask naturalists the reason; they tell you, that, were it to be raised in any place, the superior gravity of that part not being balanced, must depress it, till it meet a counterpoise (ibid.).

Similarly, '. . . it is impossible to heap up money, more than any fluid, beyond its proper level' (ibid.).

Thus, there exists a 'natural distribution of specie' among nations. This idea is not to be confused with the mercantilist doctrine that industry, especially export industry, is only necessary where there does not already exist a natural supply of precious metals; an increase in the money supply from whatever source will be illusory unless it is coupled with increased industry. Hume cites the Great Inflation:

Can one imagine, that it had ever been possible, by any laws, or even by any art or industry, to have kept all the money in Spain, which the galleons have brought from the Indies? Or that all commodities could be sold in France for a tenth of the price which they would yield on the other side of the Pyrenees, without finding their way thither, and draining from that immense treasure? (ibid.).

In Hume's account, then, changes in price levels play the predominant role in bringing about the necessary adjustment of trade balances, and the additional correcting factor of exchange rate movements is held to be of minor importance. This was a major achievement in international monetary economics which was to hold the centre stage in that field until at least the first quarter of the present century, and which has seen a recrudescence in various forms in various quarters more recently.

Nevertheless, although the Humean foundations remained intact for a century and a half, substantial additions were made to the edifice. Thornton (1802) applied the Humean framework to the disturbance entailed by a crop failure bringing about increased imports of grain. Wheatley (1807), anticipating the Keynesian concept of effective demand, argued that the fall in output would lead to a fall in general demand, thus compensating for the increased grain imports by allowing more to be exported. Ricardo (1810) also argued against Thornton but with much less cogent reasoning. His argument was that Hume's analysis could not be applied to disturbances of a non-monetary nature; not because of their tendency to be temporary. Assuming next year's crop does not fail, any adjustment of specie levels and relative prices will have to be reversed later, so why bother? Ricardo gives no real reason as to why seasonal movements of specie should be precluded.

Ricardo's most significant contribution in this area was to synthesize the law of comparative costs and the idea of a natural distribution of specie (Ricardo, 1821) with consequent implications for relative wages and prices, leaving the details to be worked out by Nassau Senior 10 years later (Senior, 1830). John Stuart Mill (1848) further elaborated this Seniorian doctrine by adding the complication of transport costs into the analysis. Moreover, although Mill accepts Hume's thesis, complete with its emphasis on movements in the terms of trade, he makes two important extensions. Firstly, and most importantly, he shows that an inflow of specie causes interest rates to decline, thus causing an outflow of capital and an exchange rate adjustment — hence grafting the foreign exchange market and the capital account on to the analysis. Mill was also one of the earliest economists to recommend the use of Bank Rate as a method of protecting reserves and exchange rates, although this idea is often credited to Gossen (1854).

In essence, then, Hume's was the balance of payments theory that economists were still working with in the 1920s and 1930s, and perhaps even up to the outbreak of the Second World War. The Marginalist revolution associated with the names of Menger, Jevons, Walras and Marshall left the thesis virtually intact. If anything, the theory was strengthened. Pigou (1932), for example, applies marginal utility functions to what is essentially a Humean analysis of the effect of war reparations on the terms of trade.

Viner, in 1937, could write:

> The 'classical' theory of the mechanism of international trade, as developed from Hume to J S Mill, is still, in its general lines, the predominant theory. No strikingly different mechanism, moreover, has yet been convincingly suggested, although there has been gain in precision of analysis, and some correction of undoubted error (1937, p. 291).

Short-run Marginalism: The Elasticities Approach

The conventional wisdom in the first quarter of this century, then, was still along distinctly Humean lines, albeit with modifications made to allow for, *inter alia*, the effects of interest rates on capital movements; a fractional reserve banking system (this was the major upshot of the so-called Bullionist controversy, see for example, Ricardo, 1810, Viner, 1937, chs III and IV); and an explicit recognition of the similarity between gold movements and changes in foreign balances. We have noted how this body of theory was left unscathed by the Marginalist revolution. Nevertheless, a (largely complementary) body of balance of payments theory did grow out of marginalism. This was essentially a short-run orientated body of analysis which became known as the 'elasticities approach' and which still survives in one form or another to the present day. The crux of this approach is embodied in a single formula.

Consider a two-country, two-good world. Let supply and demand elasticities be e_i and η_i respectively. Then it can be shown that the effect of a devaluation on country 1's balance of trade is positive if:

$$K = \frac{\eta_1 \eta_2 \, (1 + e_1 + e_2) + e_1 e_2 \, (\eta_1 + \eta_2 - 1)}{(\eta_1 + e_2) \, (\eta_2 + e_1)} > 0 \qquad (1.1)$$

(see, for example, Haberler, 1949). K is often called the 'elasticity of the balance of payments' (Metzler, 1948). In particular, from (1.1) we have:

$$\underset{\substack{e_1 \to \infty \\ e_2 \to \infty}}{\mathrm{Lim}} \, (\mathrm{sgn}\, K) = \underset{\substack{e_1 \to \infty \\ e_2 \to \infty}}{\mathrm{Lim}} \, (\mathrm{sgn}\, (\eta_1 + \eta_2 - 1)) \qquad (1.2)$$

From (1.2) we can see that, for a devaluation to improve 1's trade balance in a Keynesian model, we require:

$$(\eta_1 + \eta_2) > 1 \qquad (1.3)$$

which is normally referred to as the Marshall–Lerner condition. Expression (1.1) is usually referred to as the Robinson–Metzler equation or 'four elasticities formula'.

The elasticities approach can be seen as a way of looking for sufficient conditions for there to be a balance of payments (and hence foreign exchange market) equilibrium. The Marshall–Lerner condition is in fact a sufficient condition (assuming perfectly elastic supplies) for each country's offer curve to be monotonically decreasing (equivalent to gross substitutability), which entails that any foreign exchange market equilibrium is both unique and stable. Equivalently, it implies that the supply and demand schedules for foreign exchange do not have pathological slopes (Haberler, 1949).

The elasticities approach seems to have been discovered independently by three economists. The first exposition is by Bickerdike (1920), who makes the point that short-run demand elasticities are likely to be small and so modest balance of payments imbalances may lead to an extremely volatile foreign exchange market. Metzler (1948), following Robinson (1937), argues that Bickerdike does not take adequate account of the likelihood of the stabilizing influence of the inelasticity of short-run export supply. Joan Robinson in her celebrated essay on 'The Foreign Exchanges' (1937), derives essentially similar results to Bickerdike, although she places more emphasis on inelasticity of supply. Brown (1942) presents a broadly similar analysis, although he introduces raw materials and is generally more optimistic concerning the elasticity of export demand.

These, then, are the tools that the international monetary economist had at hand in the interwar years: the (modified) specie-flow mechanism as a long-run automatic adjustment process, and the elasticities approach springing from short-run microeconomic analysis and dealing with tiny increments of economic change. The transition to a broadly Keynesian approach was, as we shall see, the outcome of a number of empirical and theoretical anomalies in international monetary economics and in economics in general. Like all scientific revolutions, the change was gradual and was attributable to more than one writer.

We have already noted anticipations of Keynes in Wheatley and J.S. Mill; contemporary pressure for change can be seen in the work of the Swedish School and particularly in that of Bertil Ohlin (e.g. Ohlin, 1928) and the exchange between Keynes and Ohlin on the 'reparations problem' in the *Economic Journal*, 1929; see also Viner, 1937, ch. 6.

KEYNES AND AFTER

The Interwar Period: Anomalies and Revolutions

We have seen that the specie-flow mechanism was based upon a quantity theory of money and therefore implicitly accepted Say's Law of markets. This was the conventional wisdom. The large-scale chronic unemployment of the 1930s generated insuperable anomalies in the orthodoxy, culminating in the Keynesian revolution of which Keynes's *General Theory* (1936) is the central landmark. This revolution fundamentally attacked Say's Law, and hence the specie-flow mechanism. But there were other, more direct, anomalies raised in the field of international monetary economics itself which also created pressure for a fundamental shift in economists' perceptions of the balancing process.

At the instigation of Taussig, a number of empirical studies were made of the international balancing process under regimes of both fixed and floating exchange rates (Williams, 1920; Viner, 1924; White, 1933; Taussig, 1928). These investigations appeared to confirm the classical adjustment theory only too well. Taussig notes:

> The actual merchandise movements seem to have been adjusted to the shifting balance of payments with surprising exactness and speed. The process which our theory contemplates — the initial flow of specie when there is a burst of loans; the fall in prices in the lending country; the eventual increased movement of merchandise out of one and into the other — all this can hardly be expected to take place smoothly and quickly. Yet no signs of disturbance are to be observed such as the theoretic analysis previses . . . (1928, p. 239).

During the same period, a prolific number of studies were made of demand elasticities (e.g. Schultz, 1937) which yielded surprisingly low estimates. Later studies enhanced these results for demand elasticities as a whole. Hinshaw (1945), for example, produced an estimate of 0.5 for US import demand elasticity and Chang (1946) presented an estimate of 0.64 for the UK. This created a mood of 'elasticity pessimism'. Metzler observed:

> Not only did the trade balances move with surprising rapidity, but they moved in the expected direction despite the fact that the physical volume of imports is normally responsive only in a slight degree to changes in relative prices. In order to attribute the observed adjustments to changes in relative prices, it would be necessary to assume that demand elasticities are much higher than those which have actually been measured (1948, p. 215).

Thus, overemphasis on the role played by relative price changes was seen as a major defect in the classical analysis. In the words of Taussig: 'It must be confessed that here we have a phenomenon not fully understood. In part our information is insufficient; in part our understanding of other connected topics is also inadequate' (1928, p. 239).

After the publication of the *General Theory* the missing link seemed clear: that part of the adjustment process not achieved through relative price changes would be achieved through shifts in income and employment and hence in effective demand. The mechanism is, of course, well known and need not be spelt out here. Differences between Keynesian and classical explanations of balance of payments adjustment may be brought into relief via the following schema. Assume that there is, in a bilateral world, a trade imbalance in favour of country B against country A:

Keynesian Mechanism	*Classical Mechanism*
There is an injection into the circular flow of income in B (and a withdrawal from A)	There is an outflow of specie from A (and an inflow into B)
↓	↓
This leads to increased (decreased) effective demand in B (A)	This leads to a fall (increase) in prices in A (B)
↓	↓
Import demand rises (falls) in B (A) due to income effects	Import demand rises (falls) in B (A) due to substitution (and income) effects
↓	↓
Imbalance is corrected, perhaps with dampened cycles	Imbalance is corrected, perhaps with dampened cycles

In the Keynesian system, injections and withdrawals and changes in effective demand play the parts played respectively by specie flows and price changes in the classical mechanism. The advantage of the Keynesian analysis is that the world does not have to run on perfectly smooth lines as suggested by the classical mechanism: changes in effective demand can be transmitted even with rigid prices.

Multipliers and Elasticities: Some Attempts at Synthesis

As the situation stood in the 1950s, then, there were two distinct approaches to balance of payments theory: the elasticities approach and the Keynesian or international multipliers approach. Some attempts were therefore made to synthesize the two approaches as well as to remedy what were seen as the inadequacies of the elasticities approach — primarily its partial equilibrium nature. Formulators of the elasticities approach had implicitly assumed that income and prices remain constant after a devaluation, which is clearly unrealistic. Sohmen (1957), *inter alios*, had attempted to redefine the relevant elasticities as 'total' . . .

> . . . as if all adjustments caused by devaluation had been permitted to have their ultimate influence on the price–quantity relationship for the internationally traded goods (Clement *et al.*, 1967, p. 287).

Whilst this line of approach may have been theoretically expedient, it was useless for practical policy prescription as the computation of such 'total' elasticities was clearly out of the question.

More specific attempts to synthesize the Keynesian and elasticities approaches were witnessed by the publication of a series of papers in the 1950s (see, *inter alia*, Harberger, 1950; Johnson, 1956; Laursen and Matzler, 1950). These models essentially allowed the initial effects to be determined by the elasticities formula and then introduced secondary income and price effects. Clement *et al.* write:

> . . . this reformulation of the traditional elasticities approach, incorporating as it did either income elasticities or marginal or average propensities to import, gave rise to even more complex stability condition formulas . . . Nevertheless, a major advantage of this approach, in comparison with both the '*ceteris paribus*' and 'total' elasticities formulations, was that in explicitly recognizing that devaluation has significant effects beyond merely altering the exchange rate, and hence relative export and import prices, attention is directed to the roles of income effects in the devaluation mechanism (ibid.).

The major criticism levelled against these models, which Clement *et al.* dubbed the 'revised traditional variant', was their complexity. Both theoretically and empirically these models were just too messy.

At this point, mention must be made of Meade's considerable contribution to this literature. Volume I of his *Theory of International Trade* (Meade, 1952), together with its mathematical appendix, may be seen as an attempt to integrate post-Keynesian income theory with general equilibrium theory. Meade's main achievement was to draw analysis in the direction of an explicitly macroeconomic approach by recognition of the aggregate identities and relationships that hold within and between economies. In this, he was evidently much influenced by the targets-instruments analysis of Tinbergen (Tinbergen, 1952). It can be argued that Meade subsequently influenced Alexander by applying an explicitly macro approach (Alexander, 1952). Alexander essentially develops the Keynesian Aggregate Monetary Demand Identity:

$$Y \equiv C + I + G + (X - M) \tag{1.4}$$
(standard notation, real terms).

Write the balance of trade as B:

$$B \equiv X - M \tag{1.5}$$

and define (domestic) absorption A:

$$A \equiv C + I + G \tag{1.6}$$

then:

$$B \equiv Y - A \tag{1.7}$$

Alexander's analysis is based entirely on identity (1.7), which emphasizes the fundamental point that trade imbalance can only arise from a difference between domestic output and expenditure.

Taking first differences:

$$\Delta B = \Delta Y - \Delta A \qquad (1.8)$$

Now decomposing the effect of a devaluation into direct (ΔD) and indirect (via ΔY, $c\Delta Y$) effects on absorption:

$$\Delta A = c\Delta Y + \Delta D \qquad (1.9)$$

Thus, from (1.8) and (1.9):

$$\Delta B = (1 - c)\Delta Y - \Delta D \qquad (1.10)$$

Equation (1.10) directs our attention to three fundamental factors concerning the outcome of a devaluation: how the devaluation affects real income; how the propensity to absorb (c) affects the outcome; and finally how direct effects are important.

Machlup (1955, 1956) strongly criticized the absorption approach, arguing that it is nothing more than tautological reasoning based on an identity. In Chapter 3, we give an analysis of the use of identities in macro modelling and show how they can be misleading; it suffices to say here that we are basically in agreement with Machlup on this point, and see the utility of the absorption approach primarily in terms of its use as a taxonomic device. As Johnson notes:

> . . . More important and interesting is the light which this approach sheds on the policy problem of correcting a deficit, by relating the balance of payments to the overall operation of the economy rather than treating it as one sector of the economy to be analysed by itself (Johnson, 1958, p. 158).

Machlup further criticized Alexander for neglecting relative price effects. Apparently in response to Machlup's criticisms, Alexander produced a second, more rigorous, paper in which he introduced the concept of a reversal factor as the effects of a change in income brought about by the initial elasticities effect on the trade balance (Alexander, 1959). These are thus second-round effects additional to the initial impact effects.

If h and m be the marginal propensities to hoard and import respectively, an asterisk denotes a foreign variable, and v denotes the ratio m/h, then Alexander's final synthesis formula may be expressed:

$$\frac{\partial B}{\partial f} = \frac{E}{1 + v + v^*} \tag{1.11}$$

where E is a four-elasticities formula similar to (1.1).

Other attempts at synthesis include Brems (1957) and Michaely (1960). Brems works with a highly disaggregated model (38 equations), specific (Leontief) technology and other technical specificities (e.g. Cobb–Douglas demand curves). His main conclusion seems to be that a devaluation will be successful, under his assumptions, if the income effects of a price change are large relative to the substitution effects, and unsuccessful otherwise. Michaely's far less technical analysis concludes that the key to synthesis lies in the real balance effect: the devaluation leads to a change in relative prices and hence real balances and hence absorption. Michaely's stress on monetary factors as the upshot of an attempt at synthesis was symptomatic of a more general trend and foreshadowed Tsiang's paper (Tsiang, 1961) which essentially reverts to the analysis of Meade (1952) and formulates an 11-equation model of a monetary open economy. This realization of the importance of monetary factors, together with attempts to place balance of payments theory in a general equilibrium framework (e.g. Hahn, 1959) and the development of portfolio theory was to lead to the development of the so-called monetary approach to the balance of payments.

Internal and External Balance: The Policy Dilemma

Meade (1952) was among the first to consider the problem of attaining simultaneous internal (in terms of unemployment) and external (in terms of the balance of payments) balance. He showed that the conflict between internal and external balance could be reconciled if monetary and fiscal policy were used for external balance.

Swan (1963) essentially elaborated Meade's ideas and encapsulated them in the now celebrated 'Swan diagram' (Figure 1.2). On the vertical axis we have the exchange rate (units of home currency per unit of foreign currency) or terms of trade, and on the horizontal axis real expenditure. If we trace out the equilibrium loci for internal and external balance, they will have the slopes shown (under normal assumptions) and will define four 'zones of economic unhappiness' as indicated.

The implication of the diagram is that the authorities should adopt the appropriate policy mix according to which point in the diagram represents the state of the economy. Moreover, the relative slopes of the equilibrium loci depend on the precise functional forms of the model adopted and there may be a comparative advantage in assigning certain instruments to certain problems, thus solving the 'assignment problem'.

Figure 1.2   Swan's diagram

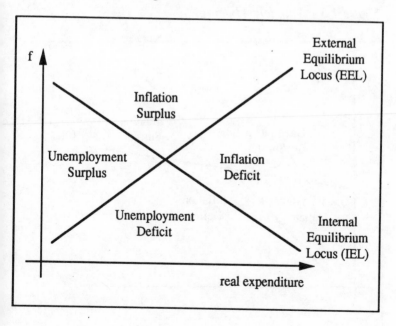

Mundell's contribution (Mundell, 1962, 1963) was much more innovative. Drawing on the Canadian experience of high international capital mobility, he pointed to the implications of the assets markets for stabilization policy. In so doing, Mundell integrated asset markets and capital mobility into open-economy macroeconomics and, in the words of Dornbusch, '. . . created models and concepts that rapidly became the Volkswagens of the field — easy to drive, reliable and sleek' (1980).

In Mundell's diagram, we have on the vertical axis monetary policy (represented by Bank Rate) and on the horizontal axis fiscal policy (represented by government expenditure). We can trace out equilibrium loci as in the Swan diagram, examine the regions of 'economic happiness' and infer a solution to the assignment problem according to the relative slopes of the schedules and our position in the state space (Figure 1.3). The relatively more efficient trade-off represented by the external equilibrium locus reflects the high interest elasticity of international capital.

Figure 1.3   Mundell's diagram

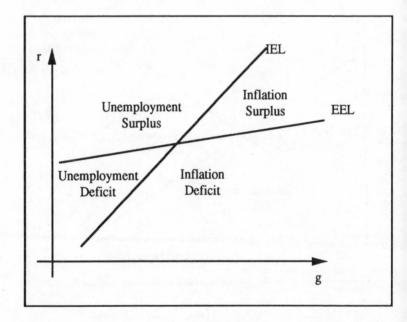

In an IS–LM framework, Mundell (1968) purported to show that the appropriate solution to the assignment problem is to react with monetary policy to the balance of payments and with fiscal policy to output and employment. Mundell's basic model consists of the following equations:

$$Y = C(Y) + I(r) + BT(Y, f) \tag{1.12}$$

$$M = L(r, Y) \tag{1.13}$$

$$B = BT(Y, f) + K(r, f) \tag{1.14}$$

where r is the interest rate, f the exchange rate, M the money supply, L the demand for money, BT the balance of trade, B the balance of payments and K represents net capital inflow. This is essentially the IS–LM model of the closed economy with unemployment and constant wages and prices, extended to the open economy in a very simple way. Takayama (1969) has shown how this model may be adjusted to handle several cases under varying assumptions. As represented in (1.12)–(1.14), it represents the standard Keynesian case of fixed wages and fixed prices. With both prices and wages flexible it becomes a very simple classical model and with wages fixed and prices flexible it is an intermediate case (see Keynes, 1936, ch. 2). Further assumptions can be made concerning the degree of capital mobility and sterilization.

In the Keynesian version under fixed rates, both fiscal and monetary policy will generally have positive effects on the level of income. Under perfect capital mobility, monetary policy becomes impotent, since any change in the interest rate leads immediately to a capital outflow and hence adjusts the effective level of the money supply. If, however, there is complete sterilization by the monetary authorities, then the degree of capital mobility does not matter for as long as such policies can be pursued.

Mundell (1968) extends this model to the analysis of two countries. Under the assumption of perfect capital mobility, most of the earlier conclusions are valid. The main differences are that an increase in government expenditure in one country raises its real income but can either raise or

lower the real income of the other country under fixed
exchange rates, whereas monetary policy raises income in
both countries.

Swoboda and Dornbusch (1973) extend the analysis to
consider any degree of capital mobility. Some of their
findings are summarized in the following quotation:

> . . . the model emphasises the importance of monetary factors in
> determining the impact of transfers and expenditure-switching
> policies on the level of world income and its distribution among
> countries. Finally, the concept of a 'natural distribution of specie'
> retains its importance even in a world of underemployment . . .
> The main point is simply that 'Hume's Law' with its monetary
> mechanism of payments adjustment holds in the face of unemploy-
> ment and wage rigidities (Swoboda and Dornbusch, 1973).

This 'back-to-Hume' conclusion is typical of much of the
literature in international monetary economics in this period.

One major criticism which has been levelled at Mundell's
approach is that it is entirely in terms of flows and so is
inconsistent with portfolio theory, which is ultimately concerned with the demand for stocks — in the presence of
uncertainty an interest rate change will lead to an equili-
brating change in portfolios rather than a perpetual flow.
The distinction between stock and flow equilibria had been
made earlier, but not fully exploited, by Johnson (1958).

In some sense, however, the work of Swan and Mundell
had been pre-empted by Salter (1958), who in fact had
already examined similar questions of internal and external
balance and had been the first to use a diagram drawn in
traded–non-traded goods space. Mention should also be made
in this connection of Pearce's contribution (Pearce, 1961).
Pearce was among the first to examine balance of payments
theory in terms of tradeables and non-tradeables (although
see Oppenheimer, 1974).

General Equilibrium Models

By the early 1960s, following the work of, *inter alios*, Meade,
Harberger and Laursen and Metzler, the standard analysis was
one of comparative statics within an explicitly macroeconomic

framework, with income demand-determined and with the exchange rate setting relative prices. Since, by way of contrast, the analysis in the pure theory of the international trade had been almost exclusively in terms of general equilibrium models, it is not surprising that attempts were made to introduce money into these models and analyse the balance of payments within this kind of general equilibrium framework.

An early contribution in this vein is Hahn (1959). In this paper, Hahn inserts two fiat currencies into a standard two-country model. His basic result is as follows:

> Assuming the goods market to be in equilibrium both before and after a change in the rate of exchange, the balance of payments of country 1) will change in the same direction as the price of currency 2) in terms of currency 1) changes provided all goods and currencies are gross substitutes (Hahn, 1959, p. 117).

Similar results were later obtained by Kemp (1962). Negishi (1968) showed that the Robinson–Metzler four-elasticities formula can be derived within a general equilibrium framework if it is assumed that all cross-price effects are zero.

The most striking result of these analyses, as in the attempts to synthesize the elasticity and Keynesian approaches, was the rediscovery of the importance of monetary factors. Another major impetus in this direction was the development of portfolio theory.

Portfolio Balance and International Capital Movements

In these analyses, the approach is focused primarily on the capital account of the balance of payments. As we have pointed out, attempts at synthesis of the Keynesian and elasticity approaches pointed up important differences arising from the explicit consideration of money. This, together with a dissatisfaction with the limitations of the analysis to the trade account, led to the application of portfolio theory in this context.

This literature is basically an elaboration of early work

done by McKinnon (1969) and McKinnon and Oates (1966) and is an extension of more general portfolio theory developed by Markowitz (1959) and Tobin (1965). Other studies which attempt to incorporate portfolio theory into general equilibrium models include Branson, 1986; Lee, 1969; Bryant and Hendershott, 1970; Branson, 1971; Hodjera, 1971; and Allen, 1973.

In these models the basic point of departure from a more traditional approach is the distinction made between stock and flow equilibria for assets. Steady-state stock equilibrium prevails when the constellation of asset prices is such that desired and actual asset holdings coincide. In this set-up, international capital flows are only temporary phenomena which bring about stock equilibrium, although flow disequilibrium can be longer lived in a growing economy with capital flows reflecting the equilibrium rate of accumulation of various assets in individual portfolios. In a Mundellian model, for example, a balance of payments deficit could be taken care of by raising domestic interest rates and attracting capital inflows — thus ensuring a flow equilibrium. Clearly, however, there will come a point where foreign investors do not wish to invest any more in the domestic economy — they will have achieved a stock equilibrium.

Although Meade, Johnson and Mundell seemed to be aware of the stock-flow distinction and commented upon it, McKinnon and Oates, 1966; McKinnon, 1969; Oates, 1965; and Ott and Ott, 1965, 1968, are the earliest analyses in which portfolio equilibrium is introduced directly by imposing a stock equilibrium constraint (for example, by requiring that the overall balance of payments on the current and capital accounts individually should be equal to zero in full equilibrium — thereby attempting to analyse the full stationary equilibrium. Later papers such as Branson, 1968; Willet, 1967; Willet and Forte, 1969; and Kouri and Porter, 1974, built on a more Tobinesque theory of portfolio choice to analyse capital movements either as a stock adjustment, which would be once-and-for-all, or as a result of differential growth rates of elements of the whole portfolio, in which case it could be continuous.

Most of this literature is concerned with analysing

short-term capital movements independently of the current account of the balance of payments. The monetary approach to the balance of payments, in explicitly attempting to capture the essential behavioural features of the whole external account by an appropriate application of the stock equilibrium approach, is in many ways an offshoot of the international portfolio balance literature, although we shall outline important differences.

The Monetary Approach to the Balance of Payments

The monetary approach to the balance of payments under fixed exchange rates (MABP) arguably finds its most succinct and articulate exposition in the collection of papers edited by Frenkel and Johnson (1976) — for an extension to the floating rate case see Frenkel and Johnson, 1978. Its line of development, however, can be traced as far back as Polak, 1957 and Johnson, 1958 and even, some authors have maintained, to the Dutch School during the interwar period (de Jong, 1973). Moreover, advocates of the monetary approach have sought to trace their intellectual lineage at least as far back as Hume (1752) (see for example, Frenkel and Johnson, 1976a; Frenkel, 1976). It is indeed true that monetary flows form the core of both the specie-flow mechanism and the MABP, and that each regards the balancing process as essentially self-regulating. In the specie-flow mechanism, however, the variables bringing about the equilibrium are relative commodity prices (this is why the theory is sometimes termed the price-specie-flow mechanism). In the MABP, the important variable is the desired level of real balances as reflected in a stable demand for money function.

The monetary approach was developed in the 1960s and early 1970s primarily by Mundell (1968, 1971) and Johnson (1972) (see also Komiya, 1969). More recent contributors are numerous and include Laidler (1972), Swoboda (1973), Dornbusch (1973), Mussa (1974), Borts and Hansen (1977), Blejer (1979) and Johannes (1981). The approach has been applied as an explanation of world-wide inflationary processes (Johnson, 1972; Whitman, 1975), to the analysis of devaluation in developing countries (Connolly and Taylor, 1976) and as a simplified theoretical basis for policy proposals by groups such as the IMF (Rhomberg and Heller, 1977). The most comprehensive survey is perhaps Kreinin and Officer, 1978.

The MABP goes much further than previous monetary analyses in that instead of just adding money into the model, monetary aspects are regarded as the very core of the analysis. As Frenkel and Johnson write, somewhat tautologically:

> The main characteristics of the monetary approach to the balance of payments can be summarised in the proposition that the balance of payments is essentially a monetary phenomenon (1976, p. 21).

The definition of the balance of payments is the starting point of any theory concerned with the external account. MABP theorists implicitly define this term to mean the set of accommodating transactions 'below the line' in the accounts. They thus take this to be a summary of all the other accounts put together. They are therefore able to draw the inference: '. . . the monetary approach should in principle give an answer no different from that provided by a correct analysis in terms of the other accounts, . . .' (Frenkel and Johnson, 1976a, p. 22).

Basically, the MABP is a supply and demand analysis of the money market in an open economy; any excess stock demand for or supply of money is exactly reflected in flows through the balance of payments. The supply of money can be seen as a multiple of the monetary base which is composed of an international reserve component and a domestic component. Only the latter is directly under the control of the monetary authorities under a fixed-rate regime. If, for example, the stock demand for money is greater than the actual money stock and the authorities do not allow the domestic component of the monetary base to rise accordingly, money will be sucked in through the external account as individuals attempt to increase their real money balances and a balance of payments surplus ensues.

Note that this account implicitly assumes a long-run, 'natural' level of output and, presumably, rapidly adjusting prices and wages, so that the hypothesized real balance effects do not affect the domestic level of economic activity. Further, most expositions assume a small open economy and perfect spatial arbitrage so that interest rates and prices are in fact determined on world markets. Naturally, the approach assumes a stable demand for money as a function of relatively few variables, often of the following form:

$$M_a = L(p, y, r) \tag{1.15}$$

If m be the money multiplier (assumed exogenously determined or constant) and R and D be the international and domestic components respectively of the monetary base, then we can write the money supply:

$$M_s = m(R + D) \tag{1.16}$$

so that in equilibrium ($M_s = M_a$);

$$L(p, y, r) = m(R + D) \tag{1.17}$$

Differentiating logarithmically and rearranging:

$$\frac{dR}{R+D} = \eta_1 \hat{p} + \eta_2 \hat{y} + \eta_3 \hat{r} - \hat{m} - \frac{dD}{R+D} \tag{1.18}$$

where a circumflex denotes a growth rate and the η_is denote the appropriate elasticities of demand for money (see Johnson, 1972). In the literature, (1.16) is referred to as the monetary base identity and (1.18) as the standard reserve flow equation. (1.18) implies (together with standard neo-classical theory) a number of comparative static effects on the balance of payments which are summarized and contrasted with standard Keynesian results in Table 1.1.

The basic message of the MABP is that, insofar as the domestic credit level is not high enough to satiate the demand for the domestic money stock, the overall balance of payments will be in disequilibrium as reflected by the trend of international reserve acquisition or loss. A corollary is that the authorities can influence the composition, but not the

Table 1.1   Effect on balance of payments
            of a rise in (cet. par.)

	y	p	r	D	m	f
Monetary	+	+	−	−	−	0
Keynesian	−	−	+	0	0	+

level, of the domestic money stock under a regime of fixed
exchange rates.

A number of other implications of the approach under
fixed rates should be noted. The first is that, since reserve
flows will only persist until there is stock equilibrium in the
money market, balance of payments problems are essentially
temporary. Secondly, they are inherently self-correcting and
although government intervention may speed up the adjustment process, it is likely to be counter-stabilizing. For
example, when the economy is running a balance of payments surplus, the authorities might attempt to sterilize the
effect of the reserve inflow on the domestic money supply
by attempting to reduce the level of domestic credit. Insofar
as this preserves the stock disequilibrium in the money
market (of which the surplus is only a symptom), imbalance
will be prolonged. Other conditions under which imbalance
may be prolonged are those of continued growth or stag-
nation. In such cases, the demand for liquidity might be
expected to fall below or outstrip changes in domestic credit;
this sort of analysis is often advanced as an explanation of
the continuous surpluses of Germany and Japan in recent
years.

The policy implications of the MABP are clear − strict
laissez-faire in international relations will always provide an
optimal, albeit long-run, solution. The only effect devaluation or commercial policy can have on the balance of
payments is through altering stock equilibria in the money
market (see Johnson, 1972; Dornbusch, 1973; Mussa, 1974).
For example, a devaluation may raise domestic prices and

hence lead to a surplus, or less of a deficit (one might also wish to outline expenditure-switching effects if a distinction is made between tradeables and non-tradeables — see Johnson, 1958). But this effect will only be transitory — once stock equilibrium is attained once more, the effects disappear. In short, the mechanism is self-equilibrating and while adroit government policy may speed up the adjustment process, the outcome will not be significantly altered.

Currie (1976) criticizes the MABP for not taking explicit account of the government budget constraint. This observation is correct and forms at least one distinction between the MABP and the related earlier literature on portfolio balance and international capital flows (e.g. McKinnon, 1969). Where the MABP literature does consider government financing constraints it is indirectly through the examination of open market operations (Frenkel and Rodriguez, 1975). Currie draws the implication that where the government runs a budget deficit, this may be fully equivalent to sterilization of a balance of payments surplus (depending on the method of finance) and so is compatible with long-run imbalance on the external account, as outlined above. In essence, the budget surplus or deficit bypasses the domestic economy and is financed through the external account. Formally he derives his results by noting that in long-run stock equilibrium capital flows must be zero, although balance of trade disequilibrium may be offset by a budget deficit or surplus. With this in mind, the long-run budget constraint is:

$$- \Delta R + T(Y') - g = 0 \qquad (1.19)$$

where Y' is the long-run level of income, $T(.)$ is the tax function and g is government expenditure (actually, Currie's budget constraint is slightly more complicated to allow for tariff revenue, but this makes no difference to the main thrust of the argument). The external constraint is:

$$\Delta R - X(Y', f) + fM(Y', f, v) = 0 \qquad (1.20)$$

where $X(.)$ is an export function, $M(.)$ is an import function

and v an expenditure-switching parameter. Adding (1.19) and
(1.20) we obtain:

$$T(Y') + fM(Y', f, v) - g - X(Y', f) = 0 \qquad (1.21)$$

Differentiating (1.21) with respect to the various policy
parameters then yields Currie's results — that in such a
scenario traditional instruments of balance of payments
correction will have long-run effects. Nobay and Johnson
(1977) argue that this analysis only applies if the authorities
are willing and able to withstand continual depletion of
reserves in the long run, or, conversely, are willing to
accumulate reserves indefinitely. If not, then the budget
must be balanced in the long run so that $(T(Y') - g)$ is zero.
From (1.19) this implies that ΔR must also be zero in the
long run, so that the aggregate constraint (1.21) cannot be
derived in that form. The value of Currie's analysis, however,
lies in bringing out the analogy between the budget constraint and the external constraint, instead of ignoring the
government sector completely or else treating it only
sketchily or implicitly.

As we have pointed out, the MABP is in many ways an
offshoot of the literature on portfolio balance and international capital flows; in some ways, however, the MABP
is more restrictive than the earlier literature. For example,
most expositions focus on the stock of real balances as the
major asset. One reason for this is the assumption of perfect
bond arbitrage; this is equivalent to assuming foreign and
domestic bonds are perfect substitutes in private portfolios,
which implies that the markets for foreign and for domestic
bonds can be considered as a single market. Explicit considerations of this market can then be avoided by an appeal
to Walras's law. Since, *ex hypothesi*, the goods and labour
markets are assumed to clear continuously (at least in the
long run), and since under fixed exchange rates the
authorities must enter the foreign exchange market to clear
it at the official parity, we need only consider equilibrium
conditions for the money market. This is essentially what the
MABP does. Further evidence for the implicit assumption

that foreign and domestic bonds are assumed to be perfect substitutes in domestic portfolios is that

> The new approach assumes — in some cases, asserts — that these monetary inflows or outflows associated with surpluses of deficits are not sterilised — or cannot be, within a period relevant to policy analysis — but instead influence the domestic money supply (Johnson, 1972).

One condition under which sterilization is impossible is precisely this perfect substitution assumption (see, for example, Obstfeld, 1982). In Chapter 4 we develop a more general portfolio balance model of the balance of payments which, whilst retaining the basic stock-flow distinction, relaxes the perfect substitutability assumption and in fact allows it to be empirically tested and in some sense measured and tracked over time using varying parameter regression methods.

Empirically, the MABP has enjoyed a reasonable amount of success. In Chapter 3, however, we give a critical appraisal of some of the empirical methods by which the theory has generally been tested.

Monetarists and Keynesians: Some Attempts at Synthesis

Frenkel *et al.* (1980) have attempted a synthesis of Keynesian and monetary approaches to the balance of payments, and Gylfason and Helliwell (1983) have extended the analysis to incorporate more general portfolio effects and allow for flexible exchange rates. The main thrust of the 1980 paper is that each of the approaches is essentially partial in nature. We might in fact paraphrase the paper by saying that the MABP concentrates on the monetary or 'LM side' of the economy whilst the Keynesian approach concentrates on the real or 'IS side', with neither approach determining prices, interest rates or equilibrium income. It would seem that the logical step is to integrate the two approaches to determine the demand side and to close the model by introducing a supply side. This is what Frenkel *et al.* attempt to do. Formally, their analysis is as follows:

$$\Delta R = p.BT(y, f/p) = K(r) \qquad (1.22)$$
$$- \quad + +$$

$$M_s = m(R + D) \qquad (1.23)$$

$$M_d = L(p, y, r) \qquad (1.24)$$
$$+ \; + \; -$$

$$M_s = M_d = M \qquad (1.25)$$

$$y = A(y, r) + g + BT(y, f/p) \qquad (1.26)$$
$$+ \; - - \; +$$

$$y = y(p) \qquad (1.27)$$
$$+$$

where:

R	=	level of international reserves;
p	=	domestic price level;
y	=	real income;
f	=	exchange rate (units of domestic currency per unit of foreign currency);
BT(.)	=	trade balance relation;
r	=	domestic interest rate;
K(.)	=	capital inflow relation;
M_s (M_d)	=	money supply (demand);
m	=	money multiplier;
D	=	domestic backing of the monetary base;
g	=	government expenditure.

Expression (1.22) is the Keynesian balance of payments equation, (1.23) is the monetary base identity and (1.24) is the money demand function, whilst (1.25) is the condition for (stock) equilibrium in the money market. Relations (1.23), (1.24) and (1.25) together constitute a set of relationships for equilibrium in the money market, and so can be used to derive the LM equation from (1.23), (1.24) and (1.25):

$$\Delta R = \Delta(1/m)L(p, y, r) - \Delta D \qquad (1.28)$$

which is the MABP reserve flow equation. Equation (1.26) is the curve and (1.27) 'is a standard supply function which can be derived from equilibrium conditions in the labour market for a given state of expectations' (Frenkel *et al.*, 1980, p. 588). Solving for p in (1.27), substituting into (1.26) and solving for r we obtain:

$$r = r(y, g, f) \qquad (1.29)$$
$$- + +$$

Substituting (1.29) into (1.22) and (1.28), we obtain respectively:

$$R = k_1 y + k_2 g + k_3 f + R_{-1} = Kn(g, f, R_{-1}) \qquad (1.30)$$
$$ + \phantom{k_1 y + k_2 g + k_3 f + R_{-1} = Kn(} + + +$$

$$R = m_1 y + m_2 g + m_3 f - D = M(g, f, D) \qquad (1.31)$$
$$ + - - - - -$$

which Frenkel *et al.* dub the K-schedule and M-schedule respectively. Plotting these in R-y space we obtain Figure 1.4, from which we can deduce a number of comparative static results, summarized in Table 1.2.

Table 1.2   Effect of changes in g, e and D on y, R, r, p and M

	dg	de	dD
dy	+	+	+
dR	?	+	−
dr	+	?	−
dp	+	+	+
dM	?	+	+

Figure 1.4 The K- and M-schedules in the Frenkel et al. synthesis

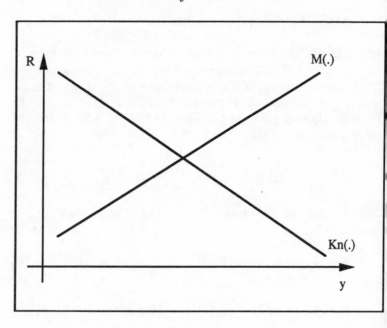

On the surface, this analysis appears to be a logically consistent and elegant synthesis. It is, however, open to the criticism that it conflates several issues, most notably the distinction between stock and flow equilibria. The ΔR in equation (1.22) and the ΔR in equation (1.28) cannot in fact be the same variable. In (1.22), for example, ΔR depends on the capital inflow relation $K(r)$, which is a flow relation and in no way depends on the equilibrium stock of assets. In (1.28), however, ΔR represents a flow necessary to bring about stock equilibrium in the money market. More fundamentally, the MABP assumes that the real side of the economy clears at levels ground out at the Walrasian equilibrium (perhaps with friction) whilst Keynesian theory assumes, for example, that there may be involuntary unemployment and that income is demand-determined. It therefore seems logically incorrect to take a set of equations from each type of model and arbitrarily mix them together.

CONCLUSION

This chapter has sketched the development of over three centuries of thought on the balance of payments. Over this period, there have been three major shifts in emphasis and approach.

Taking as our starting point the mercantilist literature, we showed how the shift to the more harmonious world-view of the classical economists mirrored a shift in moral philosophy. We characterized this shift as going from the selfish system of Hobbes to the dual sphere reconciliation of public and private interest in Smith. Apart from a more optimistic social outlook, the classicals also brought higher standards of analysis to bear on economic problems and so the specie-flow mechanism must be thought of as the first modern balance of payments theory.

The Marginalist revolution left the specie-flow mechanism virtually unscathed, although open economy analysis was supplemented by the elasticities approach. We saw, however, that the quantification afforded by the elasticities approach, coupled with the results of early demand studies, led to a mood of 'elasticity pessimism'. Other empirical work on payments imbalances suggested that the 'automatic mechanism' was working rather too well and that there may be other forces at work — rather in the way that astronomers may infer the presence of a new planet by looking at the gravitational pull on other bodies. These anomalies in the orthodoxy paved the way for revolution in international monetary economics at the same time as the existence of large-scale chronic unemployment led to a reconsideration of macroeconomics in general. The publication of Keynes's *General Theory* thus marks a watershed in international monetary economics as well as in general macroeconomics.

The post-war period has seen the third major shift in ideas in this area — from a broadly Keynesian analysis towards emphasis on the monetary aspects of payments imbalance. To some extent, this shift reflects the general prosperity of the post-war years and consequent increase in the degree of confidence that economists hold in markets. In part also the rise of the monetary approach seems to have been the outcome of a search for greater generality and consistency in the area — either through attempts to synthesize the Keynesian and elasticity approaches, through the application of general equilibrium models, or through a desire to model capital flows through the external account by the use of portfolio theory.

We noted how the pure monetary approach rested on a number of assumptions which one might in principle wish to question. Firstly, there is the assumption that the real side of the economy clears to a first approximation. This, in fact, can be seen as a major difference between Keynesian and monetary approaches to balance of payments determination and any attempt at synthesis must take account of this. This point is taken up in the next chapter. Secondly, we saw how the monetary approach implicitly assumes perfect capital mobility — or equivalently that there is a single bond market which can then be eliminated from explicit analysis by application of Walras's law. In Chapter 4 we develop a more general 'portfolio approach to the balance of payments' which relaxes this assumption and allows the level of capital mobility to vary.

2. Fix-price Equilibria in an Open Economy

INTRODUCTION

Towards the end of Chapter 1 we surveyed attempts to integrate Keynesian and monetary approaches to balance of payments theory. We argued that such attempts were virtually meaningless unless the various assumptions concerning market clearing were taken into account. This suggests that one way in which one might attempt a consistent reconciliation is through the theory of fix-price models with quantity rationing. This chapter therefore develops and analyses two fix-price models of an open economy with tradeables and non-tradeables, and with tradeables, non-tradeables and an intermediate imported good ('oil'), using an explicitly dual approach to producer behaviour. The models are extensions of the closed-economy models of Malinvaud (1977) and Barro and Grossman (1976) and are similar to those of Dixit (1978), Neary (1980) and Steigum (1980). The first model ('Mark I') is closest to that of Neary whilst the second ('Mark II') is closest to that of Steigum. However, the Mark II model is more general than any of these models and so in some sense encapsulates them all. We also derive a number of new results. However the aim of the chapter is not to create new models but to use the disequilibrium framework as a vehicle for our analysis.

It is shown that under instantaneous price adjustment the models generate results very similar to those of the monetary approach to the balance of payments models but have quite different properties in temporary equilibria with sticky prices. The taxonomy of fix-price equilibria is examined and found in some cases to be ambiguous when intermediate

43

goods are introduced; introducing intermediate goods also allows the possibility of underconsumption (in the Muellbauer–Portes, 1978, sense) even in the absence of inventory holding. The effect of an oil price shock is examined and found to be ambiguous in the most general case under standard assumptions.

THE MARK I MODEL

The setting is a small country with two aggregate commodities — non-tradeables and tradeables — one type of labour, and fiat money but no other assets. There is a given initial money supply $\bar{m}$, wage rate w and price levels p^1 and p^2 for non-tradeables and tradeables respectively. The 'small country' assumption translates into there being perfectly elastic supply and demand for the tradeable good on world markets at the going price. If f be the exchange rate and p^{2*} be the foreign currency (world) price of tradeables, then the further assumption of perfect spatial arbitrage gives $p^2 = fp^{2*}$. We assume a regime of fixed exchange rates — either fixed or on an adjustable peg regime, or sticky in a market. There are three types of agent in the economy: households, firms and government. We assume identical tastes and technology (within sectors) and abstract from distributional considerations. The analysis is thus in terms of representative agents.

Households

Households demand goods and money and supply labour. The representative unit has a consistent set of well ordered preferences satisfying the usual axioms and adequately represented by a well behaved, quasi-concave utility function:

$$u = u(x^1, x^2, H - \ell, m) \tag{2.1}$$

where x^1 = quantity of non-tradeable;
       x^2 = quantity of tradeable;

H = fixed labour endowment;
ℓ = labour supply;
m = nominal money demand (see Appendix 2.1).

This is a derived utility function, assuming that the consumer-worker's intertemporal maximization programme has been solved (e.g. by dynamic programming), contingent upon expectations up to the initial period (for a more explicit treatment of the intertemporal problem, see Appendix 2.1).

The budget constraint is:

$$p^1 x^1 + p^2 x^2 + m \leqslant w\ell + \bar{m} - t + \bar{\pi} \qquad (2.2)$$

where w = wage rate;
$\bar{m}$ = initial money balances;
$\bar{\pi}$ = last period profit;
t = government taxes (net of transfers).

Note that we assume that all profits are distributed to households in the next period.

We will write non-wage wealth, Ω:

$$\Omega = (\bar{m} - t + \bar{\pi}) \qquad (2.3)$$

Further, assuming monotonicity of consumer preferences allows the budget constraint to be binding, so that the household's maximization programme is:

$$\underset{x^1, x^2, \ell, m}{\text{Max}} \quad [u(x^1, x^2, H - \ell, m) \mid p^1 x^1 + p^2 x^2 + m = w\ell + \Omega]$$

Solving this for the indirect utility function $\Psi(p^1, p^2, w, \Omega)$ involves finding Marshallian demand functions:

$$x^1 = x^1(p^1, p^2, w, \Omega) \qquad (2.4)$$
$$ - \quad + \quad + \quad +$$

$$x^2 = x^2(p^1, p^2, w, \Omega) \qquad (2.5)$$
$$ + \quad - \quad + \quad +$$

$$\ell = \ell(p^1, p^2, w, \Omega) \qquad (2.6)$$
$$ - \quad - \quad + \quad -$$

$$\Delta m^h = m - \bar{m} = \Delta m(p^1, p^2, w, \Omega) \qquad (2.7)$$
$$\phantom{\Delta m^h = m - \bar{m} = \Delta m(} + \quad + \quad + \quad -$$

These are notional demands (negative in the case of ℓ) in the sense that the household assumes that all required quantities can be transacted at the going prices in the relevant markets (i.e. the vector (p^1, p^2, w) is assumed to clear the markets). We assume gross substitutability between tradeables and non-tradeables.

Firms

Firms belong to one (and only one) of two sectors, producing tradeables or non-tradeables. Concentration ratios in each sector are assumed to be of a low magnitude. If sector 1 be the non-tradeables sector and sector 2 the tradeables sector then output in the ith sector is governed by technology:

$$y^i = F^i(e^i) \qquad (i = 1, 2) \qquad (2.8)$$

where y^i is output of the representative unit of the ith sector, e^i is the similarly-defined demand for labour and $F^i(.)$ is given by the state of the technology. Moreover, $F^i(.)$ is assumed strictly concave and increasing monotone.

Profits in the ith sector are:

$$\pi^i = p^i y^i - we^i, \quad i = 1, 2 \qquad (2.9)$$

Since we do not allow firms to carry inventories, they are one-period agents confined to their production functions (for a relaxation of this assumption in the setting of a closed economy see Muellbauer and Portes, 1978). Their maximization programme is therefore:

$$\underset{y^i, e^i}{\text{Max}} \quad [p^i y^i - we^i \mid y^i = F^i(e^i)] \qquad (i = 1, 2).$$

Solving this yields the profit function $\pi^i(p^i, w)$ which will have the usual properties — increasing in p^i, decreasing in w and convex and linear homogeneous in the two arguments taken together.

If e^i and y^i be optimal factor input and production (i.e. labour demand and product supply) respectively, then by Hotelling's lemma:

$$y^i = \pi_p^i(p^i, w), \quad i = 1, 2 \tag{2.10}$$

$$e^i = -\pi_w^i(p^i, w) \tag{2.11}$$

where again these are notional demands in the sense that (p^1, p^2, w) is assumed to be a market-clearing price vector.

Convexity of the profit function implies that its Hessian is positive definite and in particular.

$$(\pi_{pp}, \pi_{ww}) \gg 0 \tag{2.12}$$

This implies that the notional supply and factor demand schedules (2.10) and (2.11) are respectively upward- and downward-sloping.

Linear homogeneity of the profit function implies homogeneity of degree zero of the supply function. Hence:

$$\pi_{wp}^i = -(p^i/w)\pi_{pp}^i$$

But $(p^i, w, \pi_{pp}) \gg 0$

$$\Rightarrow \pi_{wp}^i < 0 \quad i = 1, 2 \tag{2.13}$$

This implies that supply is a decreasing function of the wage level and that factor demand is an increasing function of the price level (in the relevant sector).

Government

Government preferences are exogenous. Government demands goods and pays transfers, financing these actions by levying taxes and printing money. The government budget constraint is therefore:

$$t + \Delta m^g = p^1 g^1 + p^2 g^2 \tag{2.14}$$

where g^i denotes government demand for ith sector output. We assume that the government enjoys full priority in any implicit rationing scheme which may apply at points away from the fixed point in price–wage space.

Accounting Relationships

Budget constraints of representative agents may be written:

$$-t + \bar{\pi} + w\ell - \Delta m^h - p^1 x^1 - p^2 x^2 = 0 \tag{2.15}$$

$$p^1 y^1 - we^1 - \pi^1 = 0 \tag{2.16}$$

$$p^2 y^2 - we^2 - \pi^2 = 0 \tag{2.17}$$

$$\Delta m^g + t - p^2 g^2 - p^1 g^1 = 0 \tag{2.18}$$

If we write $\pi = \pi^1 + \pi^2$, adding (2.16) and (2.17):

$$p^1 y^1 + p^2 y^2 - we^1 - we^2 - \pi = 0 \tag{2.19}$$

Adding (2.15), (2.18) and (2.19) and rearranging:

$$p^1 (y^1 - x^1 - g^1) + p^2 (y^2 - x^2 - g^2)$$
$$+ (\Delta m^g - \Delta m^h) - (\pi - \bar{\pi})$$
$$+ w(\ell - e^1 - e^2) = 0 \tag{2.20}$$

The excess of this period's profits over those of last period represents an increase in demand for nominal balances so that we may write $\Delta m^f = (\pi - \bar{\pi})$; hence:

$$\sum_{i=1}^{2} p^i (y^i - x^i - g^i) + (\Delta m^g - \Delta m^h - \Delta m^f)$$
$$+ w(\ell - e^1 - e^2) = 0 \tag{2.21}$$

Note that net excess supply of tradeables on the home market, because of the small country assumption, is the balance of trade surplus in real terms, s, say:

$$s = y^2 - x^2 - g^2 \qquad (2.22)$$

Using this and the fact that, from the government budget constraint:

$$\Delta m^g = p^1 g^1 + p^2 g^2 - t, \qquad (2.23)$$

in (2.21):

$$p^2 s = (\Delta m^h + \Delta m^f) - (p^1 g^1 + p^2 g^2 - t)$$
$$- p^1 (y^1 - x^1 - g^1) - w(\ell - e^1 - e^2) \qquad (2.24)$$

Now if we make the strong assumption that the non-tradeables and labour markets clear due, for example, to instantaneous price adjustment, then (2.24) reduces to:

$$p^2 s = \Delta m^h + \Delta m^f - (p^1 g^1 + p^2 g^2 - t) \qquad (2.25)$$

which is very similar to equations found in the literature of the monetary approach (e.g. Johnson, 1972) and in the New Cambridge literature (e.g. Cripps and Godley, 1976), and leads to similar conclusions. An increase in the overall demand for money, *ceteris paribus*, increases the balance of trade surplus. If the private sector acquisition of financial assets (which in this model means demand for nominal balances) is stable, then any increase in the budget deficit will lead to an exactly corresponding worsening of the trade balance. This is the first similarity which we note between the Walrasian model and the monetary approach.

Notional Equilibrium with Fixed Rates

In this section we retain the assumption of clearing labour and non-tradeables markets, so that there is no rationing in the economy. We wish to trace out a labour market equilibrium locus (LMEL) in (w, p^1) space. Equating labour supply and demand:

$$\ell(p^1, p^2, w, \Omega) + \pi^1_w(p^1, w) + \pi^2_w(p^2, w) = 0 \qquad (2.26)$$

We adopt the convention of denoting the partial derivative of a variable by a subscript and in particular the derivative with respect to p^i by subscript i, e.g. $\ell_i = \frac{\partial \ell}{\partial p^i}$.

Totally differentiating (2.26), allowing only w and p^1 to change, it can easily be shown:

$$\frac{dw}{dp^1}\Big|_{LE} = \frac{\ell_1 + \pi^1_{w1}}{-(\pi^1_{ww} + \pi^2_{ww}) - \ell_w} \qquad (2.27)$$

Now, $\ell_1 < 0; \pi^1_{w1} < 0; \pi^i_{ww} > 0; \ell_w > 0$.

So (2.27) is positive and the LMEL is upward-sloping in (w, p^1) space.

Now consider the non-traded goods market equilibrium locus (NTEL) in (w, p^1) space. Equating supply and demand for non-tradeables:

$$g^1 + x^1(p^1, p^2, w, \Omega) - \pi^1_1(p^1, w) = 0 \qquad (2.28)$$

From (2.28) it is easily shown:

$$\frac{dw}{dp^1}\Big|_{NTE} = \frac{x^1_1 - \pi^1_{11}}{\pi^1_{1w} - x^1_w} \qquad (2.29)$$

Since, $x^1_1 < 0; \pi^1_{11} > 0; \pi^1_{1w} < 0; x^1_w > 0$, $\dfrac{dw}{dp^1}\Big|_{NTE} > 0$,

so the NTEL is upward-sloping in (w, p^1) space.

For given exchange rate and world prices, the intersection of LMEL and NTEL determines the equilibrium price–wage constellation. In a rectangular Cartesian coordinate system with w as ordinate and p^1 as abscissa, the open set bounded below (above) by NTEL exhibits excess demand (supply) for non-tradeables, whilst the open set bounded below (above) by LMEL displays excess supply (demand) for labour.

The existence, uniqueness and stability of general equilibrium are assumed here. We thus assume that NTEL and LMEL intersect once and once only and that NTEL is steeper than LMEL in the neighbourhood of the intersection (Figure 2.1).

Figure 2.1   The labour market and non-tradeable goods market equilibrium loci

(esl (edl) = excess supply of (demand for) labour; esnt (ednt) = excess supply of (demand for) non-tradeable)

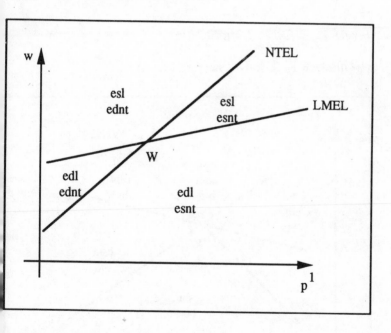

Now consider the balance of trade equilibrium locus (BTL) in (w, p^1) space. Setting the real balance of trade surplus equal to zero:

$$s = y^2 - x^2 - g^2 = 0$$

or $\pi_2^2(p^2, w) - x^2(p^1, p^2, w, \Omega) - g^2 = 0$ (2.30)

Totally differentiating (2.30), allowing only p^1 and w to change, it can be shown:

$$\frac{dw}{dp^1}\bigg|_{BT} = \frac{x_1^2}{(\pi_{2w}^2 - x_w^2)} \tag{2.31}$$

Now, $x_1^2 > 0$; $x_w^2 > 0$; $\pi_{2w}^2 < 0$, so $\dfrac{dw}{dp^1}\bigg|_{BT} < 0$,

so BTL is downward-sloping in (w, p^1) space.

Figure 2.2   General equilibrium

(bts (btd) = balance of trade surplus (deficit))

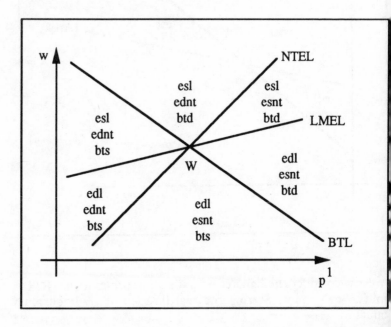

With w as ordinate and p^1 as abscissa, the open set bounded below (above) by BTL exhibits balance of trade deficit (surplus). The BTL will intersect LMEL and NTEL at the general equilibrium W (simultaneous internal and external balance (Figure 2.2).

Comparative Statics in the Walrasian Model

Devaluation

With given world prices of tradeables p^{2*} and given $p^2 = fp^{2*}$, a devaluation (increase in f) entails an increase in the home price of tradeables, from an initial level of p_o^2 say, to a level of p_1^2:

$$p_o^2 = f_o p^{2*}$$

$$p_1^2 = f_1 p^{2*}$$

$$(p_1^2, f_1) \gg (p_o^2, f_o)$$

We assume tradeables and non-tradeables to be gross substitutes; a devaluation will thus have an expenditure-switching (substitution) effect in favour of non-tradeables as well as an expenditure-reducing (income) effect. Also, since $\pi_2^2(p^2, w) > 0$ there will be a tendency for resources to switch to production of tradeables and away from production of non-tradeables. Informally, we can write NTEL:

$$N(p^1, p^2, w, \Omega, g^1) = 0 \qquad (2.32)$$
$$- \quad + \quad + \quad + \quad +$$

and see that for given w, Ω and g^1, a devaluation requires an increase in p^1 for equilibrium to be maintained, i.e. NTEL shifts to the right in (w, p^1) space.

From (2.26) we can write the LMEL as:

$$L(p^1, p^2, w, \Omega) = 0 \qquad (2.33)$$
$$- \quad - \quad + \quad -$$

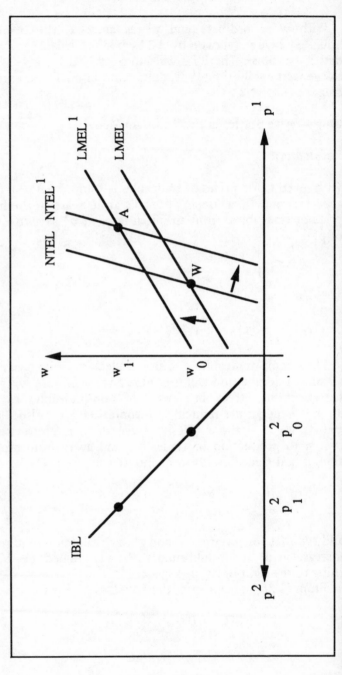

Figure 2.3   The internal balance locus

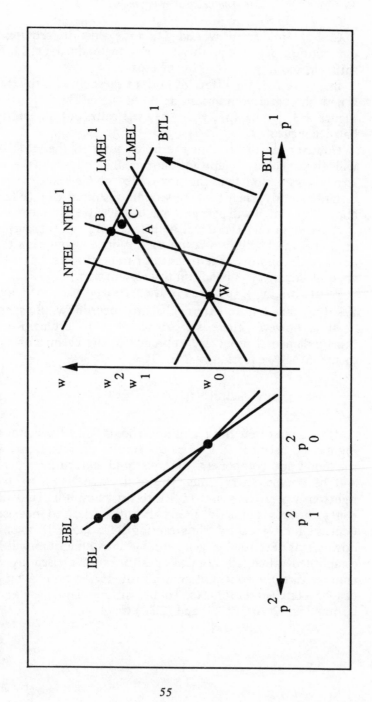

Figure 2.4 The internal and external balance loci

Clearly, for given w and Ω, a devaluation requires a reduction in p^1 for equilibrium to be maintained, i.e. LMEL shifts up and to the left in (w, p^1) space.

In Figure 2.3, the effect of both of these shifts is to attain a new short-run equilibrium at A. In the left-hand panel of Figure 2.3, points (p_o^2, w_o), (p_1^2, w_1) trace out an internal balance locus.

However, an increase in the home price of the tradeable will also involve an upward shift in BTL. If we make the strong assumption that the non-traded goods market clears instantaneously, then the intersection of shifted BTL (BTL^1) and NTEL^1 at B will give external balance. We assume that B is above A so that there will be balance of payments surplus at short-run equilibrium A, on the intuitive assumption that devaluation improves the balance of trade (Figure 2.4). (The analysis in no way depends on this assumption.)

Points (p_o^2, w_o), (p_1^2, w_2) in the left-hand panel of Figure 2.4 thus trace out an external balance locus in (w, p^2) space.

At A, however, there is a balance of trade surplus. Recall the fundamental monetary approach to the balance of payments (MABP) equation (2.25):

$$p^2 s = \Delta m^h + \Delta m^f - (p^1 g^1 + p^2 g^2 - t)$$

This implies that firms and households will be accumulating money balances so long as the surplus persists. Hence Ω, the non-wage component of household purchasing power, will be growing over time. This will cause NTEL to drift rightwards over time, and LMEL to drift upwards. Thus IBL shifts upwards. Similarly, monetary inflows lead to increased demand for tradeables, thus causing BTL and EBL to shift downwards. Eventually, general long-run equilibrium will be established when all nominal quantities have risen by an amount directly concomitant with the devaluation. A proof can be sketched as follows. Totally differentiating the equilibrium loci (2.26), (2.28) and (2.30) we obtain:

$$\begin{bmatrix} (x_1^1 - \pi_{11}^1) & (x_w^1 - \pi_{1w}^1) & x_\Omega^1 \\ (\ell_1 + \pi_{w1}^1) & (\ell_w + \pi_{ww}^1 + \pi_{ww}^2) & \ell_\Omega \\ -x_1^2 & (\pi_{2w}^2 - x_w^2) & -x_\Omega^2 \end{bmatrix} \begin{bmatrix} dp^1 \\ dw \\ d\Omega \end{bmatrix} =$$

$$- \begin{bmatrix} x_2^1 \\ (\ell_2 + \pi_{w2}^2) \\ (\pi_{22}^2 - x_2^2) \end{bmatrix} dp^2$$

This implies:

$$\begin{bmatrix} (x_1^1 - \pi_{11}^1)p^1 & (x_w^1 - \pi_{1w}^1)w & x_\Omega^1 \Omega \\ (\ell_1 + \pi_{w1}^1)p^1 & (\ell_w + \pi_{ww}^1 + \pi_{ww}^2)w & \ell_\Omega \Omega \\ -x_1^2 p^1 & (\pi_{2w}^2 - x_w^2)w & -x_\Omega^2 \Omega \end{bmatrix} \begin{bmatrix} \hat{p}^1 \\ \hat{w} \\ \hat{\Omega} \end{bmatrix} =$$

$$- \begin{bmatrix} x_2^1 p^2 \\ (\ell_2 + \pi_{w2}^2)p^2 \\ (\pi_{21}^2 - x_2^2)p^2 \end{bmatrix} \hat{p}^2$$

where a circumflex denotes proportional change.

More compactly:

$$A \, \delta = \epsilon \, \hat{p}^2$$

If Δ be the determinant of A and Δ_i be the determinant of A with the ith column replaced by ϵ, then by Cramer's rule:

$$\hat{p}^1 = (\Delta_1/\Delta)\hat{p}^2; \quad \hat{w} = (\Delta_2/\Delta)\hat{p}^2; \quad \hat{\Omega} = (\Delta_3/\Delta)\hat{p}^2.$$

Now, using the homogeneity of the equilibrium loci, Euler's theorem and standard properties of determinants it can easily be shown that

$$(\Delta_i/\Delta) = 1 \quad , \quad (i = 1, 2, 3) \text{ (QED)}.$$

In Figure 2.4 the long-run equilibrium will be at point C. This long-run neutrality is in direct accordance with the monetary approach to the balance of payments.

An increase in the money supply

Say there is a helicopter drop of money thereby leading to a once-for-all exogenous increase in wealth Ω. By similar reasoning to the devaluation case, this will lead to a rightward shift of the NTEL, a leftward shift of the LMEL and a leftward shift of the BTL. The new short-run equilibrium at the intersection of LMEL and NTEL will thus be to the right of BTL, i.e. there is a trade deficit which will continuously deplete the money stock and bring about adjustment towards long-run equilibrium. The new long-run equilibrium will be at a point where all domestic nominal variables have increased in proportion commensurate with the increase in the money stock. (To prove this formally, totally differentiate the equilibrium loci holding p^2 constant and then proceed as in the devaluation case.) As we should expect, this is precisely as predicted by the pure monetary approach to the balance of payments.

Rationing with Fixed Exchange Rates

At points away from the fixed point W in (w, p^1) space, in the absence of instantaneous price adjustment or recontracting, there will be rationing on domestic markets. Consider points on NTEL in the open set bounded below by LMEL; this exhibits excess supply of labour.

Following Clower, we posit that the household's dual decision in the face of labour rationing involves recalculation of its demand for goods, and in particular non-tradeables, the demand constraint $\bar{\ell}$ figuring as an explicit argument:

$$\tilde{x}^1 = \tilde{x}^1(\bar{\ell}; p^1, p^2, w, \Omega), \tag{2.34}$$

where $\tilde{x}^i$ denotes labour-constrained demand for the ith sector good. In fact, since the constraint is binding, income allocation replaces labour supply as a decision variable at the margin, so we might write:

$$\tilde{x}^1 = \tilde{x}^1(p^1, p^2, L, \Omega),$$

where $L = w\bar{\ell}$ = labour income, resembling the Keynesian consumption function.

Clearly we will have $\tilde{x}^1 < x^1$ almost everywhere. Hence, we may write the NTEL in the region of excess supply of labour (NTEL(ESL)) as:

$$g^1 + \tilde{x}^1(\bar{\ell}; p^1, p^2, w, \Omega) - \pi_1^1(p^1, w) = 0 \qquad (2.35)$$

Since $\tilde{x}^1 < x^1$, the region of excess demand for non-tradeables bounded by this section of NTEL will contract (Figure 2.5).

Figure 2.5   The effect of excess labour supply on
*   non-tradeable goods market equilibrium*

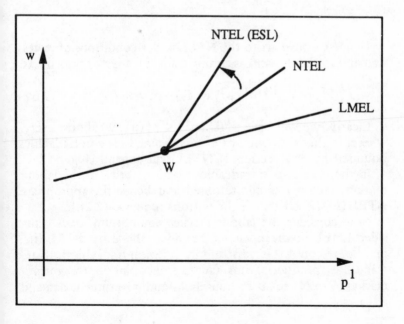

When we consider the section of NTEL in the open set bounded above by LMEL, our results depend crucially on the rationing scheme that distributes the available supply of labour between the tradeables and non-tradeables sectors. In the first instance, we examine the two polar cases of traded sector and non-traded sector priority.

If the tradeables sector enjoys priority in the labour market, then the non-tradeables sector may encounter rationing in that market. The appropriate analytic tool is thus the restricted profit function (or revenue function) defined as:

$$\tilde{\pi}^1(\bar{e}^1; p^1) = \underset{y^1}{\text{Max}} \ [p^1 y^1 \mid y^1 = F^1(\bar{e}^1)] \qquad (2.36)$$

where $\bar{e}^1 = \bar{\ell} + \pi_w^2(y^2, w)$, i.e. the total labour ration, less sector 2's demand for labour. The properties of $\tilde{\pi}^1(.)$ are standard (see McFadden, 1978): linear homogeneous and convex in p^1 in particular. Moreover, by the envelope theorem:

$$\tilde{\pi}_1^1(\bar{e}^1; p^1) = y^1$$

Hence we may write the NTEL under conditions of excess demand for labour and assuming tradeables sector priority as:

$$\tilde{\pi}_1^1(\bar{e}^1; p^1) - x^1(p^1, p^2, w, \Omega) - g^1 = 0 \qquad (2.37)$$

Clearly, we will have $\tilde{\pi}_1^1(\bar{e}^1; p^1) < \pi_1^1(p^1, w)$ almost everywhere, so that the region of excess demand for non-tradeables bounded by this section of NTEL will expand (Figure 2.6).

In the case of non-tradeables sector priority in the labour market, sector 1 is not rationed and hence the appropriate NTEL (EDL) schedule is the notional one, i.e. (2.28).

Now consider the labour market equilibrium locus. Consider LMEL in the open set bounded above by NTEL (i.e. in the region of excess supply of non-tradeables). Non-tradeables producers thus face a constraint in the output market, $\bar{y}^1$ say, equal to household and government demand

Figure 2.6   The effect of excess labour demand on non-tradeable goods market equilibrium

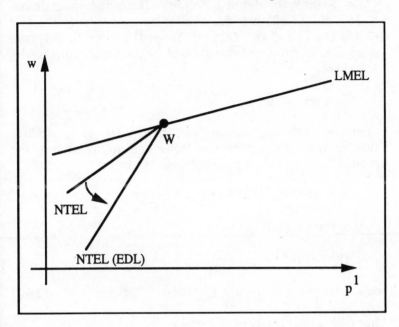

for non-tradeables. The appropriate analytic tool is thus the cost function, defined as:

$$C^1(w, \bar{y}^1) = \underset{e^1}{\text{Min}}\,[we^1 \mid F^1(e^1) = \bar{y}^1] \qquad (2.38)$$

This will be increasing, concave and linear homogeneous in w. Moreover by the envelope theorem:

$$e^1 = C^1_w(w, \bar{y}^1) \quad \text{(Shephard's Lemma)}.$$

Hence we may write the LMEL (ESNT):

$$C^1_w(w, \bar{y}^1) - \pi^2_w(p^2, w) - \ell(p^1, p^2, w, \Omega) = 0 \qquad (2.39)$$

Now because firms are one-period agents they are confined to their production functions. Thus, if they are constrained in *both* the goods market and the labour market (of which situation (2.37) and (2.39) represent limiting cases), then $y^1 = F^1(e^1)$ (as defined before). Thus, the programmes (2.36) and (2.38) are the dual of each other and the loci (2.37) and (2.39) are identical. To see this more clearly, consider that if firms are constrained in the output market by $\bar{y}^1$, where

$$\bar{y}^1 = x^1(.) + g^1$$

then they will only demand just enough labour to produce that amount. Since, with one factor and no inventories, the production function is invertible, we can write:

$$e^1 = (F^1)^{-1}(x^1(.)) + g^1),$$

so that the LMEL (ESNT) is:

$$(F^1)^{-1}(x^1(.) + g^1) - \pi_w^2(.) - \ell(.) = 0$$

or $\quad F^1(\pi_w^2(.) + \ell(.)) - x^1(.) - g^1 = 0 \qquad (2.40)$

But with a labour ration, $\bar{e}^1$, where:

$$\bar{e}^1 = \ell(.) + \pi_w^2(.),$$

(2.40) is also the NTEL (EDL).

The upshot of all this is that when tradeables' producers enjoy priority in the labour market, the whole region of simultaneous excess demand for labour and excess supply of non-tradeables ('underconsumption') vanishes — producers cannot be rationed in both markets simultaneously.

If we assume that non-tradeables' producers enjoy priority in labour markets, then NTEL (EDL) is the notional NTEL (sector 1 producers are unrationed), i.e. (2.28), which is distinct from (2.39) so that underconsumption can prevail (non-tradeables' producers are rationed in the output market, tradeables' producers in the labour market).

Now consider LMEL in the open set bounded below by NTEL, i.e. in the region of excess demand for non-tradeables.

Households, finding themselves rationed in the goods market, will recalculate their labour supply, expressing effective supply:

$$\tilde{\ell}(\bar{x}^1; p^1, p^2, w, \Omega) < \ell(p^1, p^2, w, \Omega) \qquad \text{(almost every-}$$
where)

where $\bar{x}^1 = \pi_1^1(p^1, w) - g^1$.

Hence the LMEL (EDNT) is:

$$\tilde{\ell}(\bar{x}^1; p^1, p^2, w, \Omega) + \pi_w^1(p^1, w) + \pi_w^2(p^2, w) = 0$$

Since $\tilde{\ell} < \ell$, the region of excess demand for labour will expand (Figure 2.7). Putting our observations together, we obtain Figures 2.8 and 2.9.

Figure 2.7   The effect of excess demand for non-tradeables on labour market equilibrium

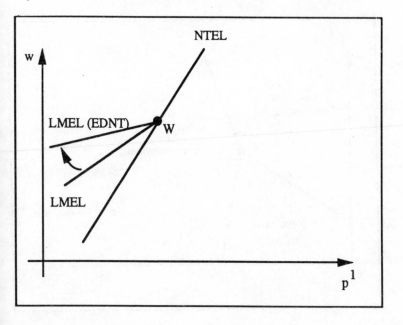

For simplicity, we assume that the tradeables sector enjoys priority when there is rationing in the labour market. We can now gather together the expressions for the various equilibrium loci for future reference:

NTEL (ESL) $\quad g^1 + \tilde{x}^1(\bar{\ell}; p^1, p^2 . w . \Omega) = \pi_1^1(p^1, w) = 0$
$$\tag{2.41}$$

$\left\{\begin{array}{l} \text{NTEL (EDL)} \\ \text{LMEL (ESNT)} \end{array}\right. g^1 + x^1(p^1, p^2, w, \Omega) - F^1(\ell(p^1, p^2, w, \Omega)$
$$+ \pi^2(p^2, w)) = 0 \tag{2.42}$$

LMEL (EDNT) $\quad \ell(\bar{x}^1; p^1, p^2, w, \Omega) + \pi_w^1(p^1, w)$
$$+ \pi_w^2(p^2, w) = 0 \tag{2.43}$$

where, in (2.41),

Figure 2.8   Regions of temporary equilibria (assuming tradeables sector priority in the labour market)

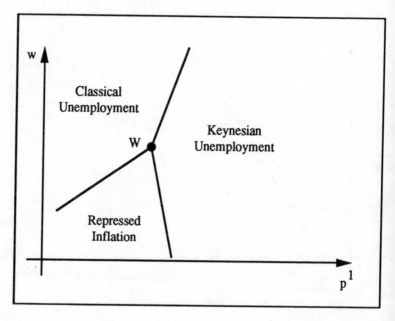

$$\bar{\ell} = -\pi_w^1(p^1, w) - \pi_w^2(p^2, w); \qquad (2.44)$$

and in (2.43):

$$\bar{x}^1 = \pi_1^1(p^1, w) - g^1 \qquad (2.45)$$

We can now look more closely at the slopes of these loci in (w, p^1) space.

Totally differentiating (2.41), using (2.44) and allowing only w and p^1 to change:

$$-\tilde{x}_\ell^1(\pi_{p1}^1 dp^1 + \pi_{ww}^1 dw + \pi_{ww}^2 dw) + \tilde{x}_1^1 dp^1 + \tilde{x}_w^1 dw$$

$$-\pi_{11}^1 dp^1 - \pi_{1w}^1 dw = 0.$$

Figure 2.9   Regions of temporary equilibria (assuming non-tradeables sector priority in the labour market)

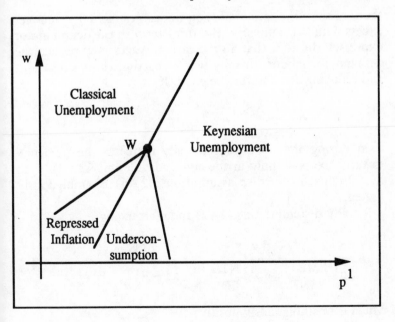

$$=> \quad \frac{dw}{dp^1}\bigg|_{\substack{NTE \\ ESL}} = \frac{\pi^1_{11} - \tilde{x}^1_1 + \tilde{x}^1_\ell \pi^1_{w1}}{\tilde{x}^1_w - \pi^1_{1w} - \tilde{x}^1_\ell(\pi^1_{ww} + \pi^2_{ww})} \qquad (2.46)$$

Now if we were to consider only the first two terms in the numerator and the denominator, (2.46) would be un-ambiguously positive. The first two terms in the numerator capture the idea that an increase in price leads to excess supply, whilst the corresponding terms in the denominator show that a wage increase will reduce supply and increase demand, thereby reducing the excess supply. The third term in the numerator shows that an increase in price will increase the demand for labour and this will have an effect on the demand for the good. Neary and Roberts (1980) have shown that $\tilde{x}^1_\ell$ may be signed unambiguously as positive, so that this term implies that an increase in prices, by relaxing the labour constraint a little, may increase demand. If

$$-\tilde{x}^1_\ell \pi^1_{w1} > \pi^1_{11} - \tilde{x}^1_1$$

then raising the price of non-tradeables actually induces excess demand. Similarly, the third term in the denominator expresses the idea that an increase in wages may reduce the demand for labour, thereby worsening the labour constraint and reducing demand for the good. If

$$\tilde{x}^1_\ell(\pi^1_{ww} + \pi^2_{ww}) > \tilde{x}^1_w - \pi^1_{1w}$$

then raising the wage level actually increases the tendency towards excess supply in the non-tradeables market. Thus, in the absence of further assumptions (2.46) is ambiguously signed.

Totally differentiating (2.42) and rearranging:

$$\frac{dw}{dp^1}\bigg|_{\substack{LME \\ ESNT}} = \frac{dw}{dp^1}\bigg|_{\substack{NTE \\ EDL}} = \frac{F^1_e \ell_1 - x^1_1}{x^1_w - F^1_e \ell_w - F^1_e \pi^2_{ww}} \qquad (2.47)$$

which is unambiguously positive.

Totally differentiating (2.43), allowing only w and p^1 to change and using (2.45), we can show:

$$\frac{dw}{dp^1}\Bigg|_{\substack{\text{LME} \\ \text{EDNT}}} = \frac{-(\pi^1_{w1} + \tilde{\ell}_1 + \tilde{\ell}_x \pi^1_{11})}{\tilde{\ell}_w + (\pi^1_{ww} + \pi^2_{ww}) + \tilde{\ell}_x \pi^1_{1w}} \qquad (2.48)$$

Now we already have:

$$\pi^1_{w1} < 0; \quad \pi^1_{11} > 0; \quad \pi^i_{ww} > 0, (i = 1, 2);$$

while standard consumer theory yields:

$$\tilde{\ell}_1 < 0; \tilde{\ell}_w > 0.$$

Neary and Roberts (1980) have shown that the effect of relaxing a goods market constraint on labour supply is ambiguous. A relaxation of the goods ration has a substitution and an income effect on labour supply which work in opposite directions if consumption and leisure are normal and net substitutes. The substitution effect of the relaxation of the goods constraint tends to reduce demand for leisure (a net substitute for goods), thereby raising labour supply. But the income effect of the relaxation tends to increase the demand for leisure and so to reduce labour supply, and this effect will be larger the further we are from equilibrium (see Neary and Roberts, 1980, pp. 38–9). Thus, the sign of $\tilde{\ell}_x$ is ambiguous.

However, in the light of these remarks we might hazard the following assumptions. Near equilibrium (substitution effect dominant):

$$\tilde{\ell}_x > 0, \text{ but small,}$$

far from equilibrium (income effect dominant):

$$\tilde{\ell}_x < 0.$$

Using these assumptions, we see that near equilibrium $\tilde{\ell}_x$

Figure 2.10 Regions of temporary equilibria

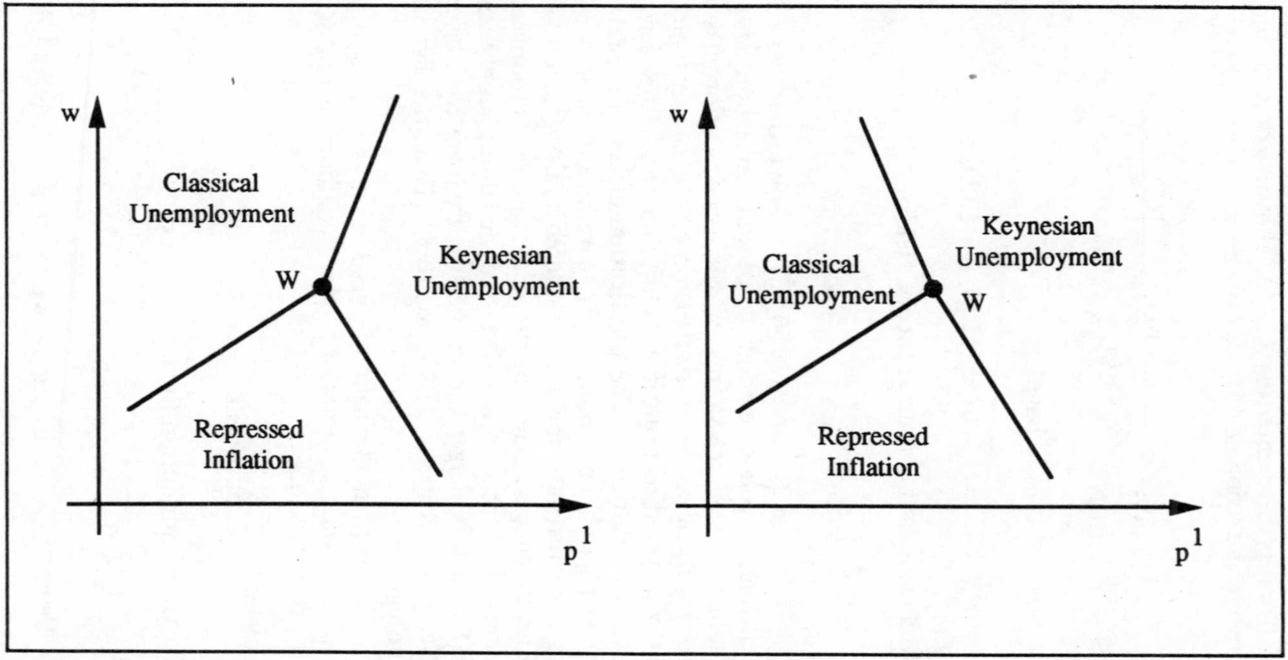

68

is insignificant in (2.48), although positive, so that (2.48) may be thought of as positively signed. Far from equilibrium, however, $\tilde{\ell}_x$ becomes negative, so that (2.48) may be unambiguously signed as positive.

We are now in a position to redraw Figure 2.9, taking explicit account of the above analysis. The result is Figure 2.10.

Figure 2.10 reflects the ambiguity of the slope of NTEL under excess supply of labour. This slope may be quite important for the resolution of a number of problems. For example, it is unclear whether an increase in the wage level (from a point of Walrasian equilibrium) will send the economy into a regime of classical or of Keynesian unemployment. Thus, Malinvaud's contention that classical unemployment is a result of too high a real wage level (Malinvaud, 1977, p. 85) may or may not be true in this context.

Comparative Statics in Keynesian Unemployment: Devaluation

In order to contrast the properties of the Walrasian model (which we showed to be essentially equivalent to the monetary approach to the balance of payments), we now consider the effects of devaluation on the trade balance in a Keynesian unemployment scenario.

Under Keynesian unemployment there is excess supply of non-tradeables and labour. Demand for tradeables is given by

$$\tilde{x}^2 = \tilde{x}^2(\bar{\ell}, p^1, p^2, w, \Omega) \tag{2.49}$$

where $\bar{\ell}$ is the labour ration

$$\bar{\ell} = C_w^1(w, \bar{y}^1) - \pi_w^2(p^2, w) \tag{2.50}$$

and

$$\bar{y}^1 = \tilde{x}^1(\ell, p^1, p^2, w, \Omega) + g^1 \tag{2.51}$$

The nominal trade balance is therefore given by

$$B = p^2 s = p^2 \pi_2^2(p^2, w) - p^2 \tilde{x}^2(\bar{\ell}, p^1, p^2, w, \Omega) - p^2 g^2$$

$$(2.52)$$

Hence $\dfrac{dB}{dp^2} = p^2(\pi_{22}^2 - \tilde{x}_2^2) - p^2 \tilde{x}_\ell^2 \, \bar{\ell}_2$ (assuming initially balanced trade)

$$\Rightarrow \frac{dB}{dp^2} = p^2(\pi_{22}^2 - \tilde{x}_2^2) - p^2 \tilde{x}_\ell^2 \, \frac{C_{wy}^1 \tilde{x}_2^1 - \pi_w^2{}_2}{1 - C_{wy}^1 \tilde{x}_\ell^1} \qquad (2.53)$$

The first and second terms on the RHS of (2.53) represent direct output and demand effects of the increase in the home price of tradeables and together tend to increase the trade balance. The third term on the RHS represents a general equilibrium multiplier effect of the price change on the labour ration and hence demand for tradeables. Firstly, the increased tradeables output raises labour demand. Secondly, the expenditure-switching effect relaxes a little the demand constraint on non-tradeables and so again raises employment. The consequent relaxation of the labour demand ration will thus raise home demand for tradeables and will tend to worsen the trade balance.

If (2.53) is to be positive, then:

$$\frac{(\pi_{22}^2 - \tilde{x}_2^2)(1 - C_{wy}^1 \tilde{x}_\ell^1) - \tilde{x}_\ell^2 (C_{wy}^1 \tilde{x}_2^1 - \pi_w^2{}_2)}{(1 - C_{wy}^1 \tilde{x}_\ell^1)} > 0$$

From this expression it is easy to derive:

$$\frac{(\sigma_2^2 + \epsilon_2^2)(1 - \epsilon_{y1}^\ell \epsilon_\ell^1) + \epsilon_\ell^2 (\epsilon_2^\ell - \epsilon_{y1}^\ell \epsilon_2^1)}{(1 - \epsilon_{y1}^\ell \epsilon_\ell^1)} > 0 \qquad (2.54)$$

where:

σ_2^2 = own-price elasticity of supply of tradeables
$\quad\quad (= (p^2/y^2)\pi_{22}^2)$;

ϵ_2^2 = own-price elasticity of demand for tradeables
$\quad\quad (= -(p^2/y^2)\tilde{x}_2^2)$;

$\epsilon_{y^1}^{\ell}$ = elasticity of labour demand with respect to the non-tradeables demand constraint $(= (\bar{\ell}/\bar{y}^1)C_{wy}^1)$;

ϵ_{ℓ}^1 = elasticity of demand for non-tradeables with respect to the labour constraint $(= (\bar{y}^1/\bar{\ell})\tilde{x}_{\ell}^1)$;

ϵ_2^{ℓ} = elasticity of demand for labour with respect to the price of non-tradeables $(= -(p^2/\bar{\ell})\pi_{w2}^2)$;

ϵ_{ℓ}^2 = elasticity of demand for tradeables with respect to the labour constraint $(= (\bar{\ell}/y^2)\tilde{x}_{\ell}^2)$.

Expression (2.54) is a 'six elasticities formula' analogous to the familiar Robinson–Metzler four elasticities formula discussed in Chapter 1. In the notation of this section, letting an asterisk denote a foreign variable, the Robinson–Metzler condition is:

$$\frac{\epsilon_2^2\epsilon_2^{2*}(1 + \sigma_2^2 + \sigma_2^{2*}) + \sigma_2^2\sigma_2^{2*}(\epsilon_2^2 + \epsilon_2^{2*} - 1)}{(\epsilon_2^2 + \sigma_2^{2*})(\epsilon_2^{2*} + \sigma_2^2)} > 0$$

In the present model we have assumed both σ_2^{2*} and ϵ_2^{2*} to be infinite, so that the Robinson–Metzler condition reduces to

$$\epsilon_2^2 + \sigma_2^2 > 0 \tag{2.55}$$

In the derivation of the Robinson–Metzler condition, no account has been taken of the labour market. Setting all labour demand elasticities in our six elasticities formula equal to zero, we obtain (2.55). This shows that the Robinson–Metzler formula is more general than our six elasticities formula in that no 'small country' assumption is made, but that the six elasticities formula is more general than the Robinson–Metzler condition in that allowance is made for the full general equilibrium impact of the devaluation, including those acting through the labour market.

THE MARK II MODEL

Extensions

We now extend the analysis by allowing a wholly imported intermediate good ('oil') to be used in the production of tradeables and non-tradeables. The world price of oil is v^* and so domestic price v is given by $v = fv^*$. Let the amount of oil used in sector i be z^i ($i = 1, 2$). Then we may rewrite equation (2.8):

$$y^i = F^i(e^i, z^i) \quad (i = 1, 2) \tag{2.8'}$$

with $\quad F^i_e > 0; F^i_z > 0; F^i_{ee} < 0; F^i_{zz} < 0.$

Profit is given by:

$$\pi^i = p^i y^i - we^i - vz^i \tag{2.9'}$$

and the maximization programme becomes:

$$\underset{y^i, e^i, z^i}{\text{Max}} \quad [p^i y^i - we^i - vz^i \mid y^i = F^i(e^i, z^i)] \quad (i = 1, 2)$$

This yields the profit function $\pi^i(p^i, w, v)$, which will be increasing in p^i, decreasing in w and in v, and convex and linear homogeneous in all three arguments taken together.

By convexity:

$$(\pi^i_{ii}, \pi^i_{ww}, \pi^i_{vv}) \gg 0 \quad (i = i, 2)$$

By homogeneity:

$$p^i \pi^i_{ii} + w\pi^i_{iw} + v\pi^i_{iv} = 0$$

but

$$(p^i, w, v, \pi^i_{ii}) \gg 0$$

hence, by symmetry:

$$(\pi^i_{iw}, \pi^i_{iv}) \ll 0$$

Also by homogeneity:

$$p^i\pi^i_{iv} + w\pi^i_{vw} + v\pi^i_{vv} = 0$$

but:

$$(p^i, w, v, \pi^i_{vv}) \gg 0 \text{ and } \pi^i_{iv} < 0$$

so the sign of π^i_{vw} ($= \pi^i_{wv}$) is ambiguous.

Consider therefore the problem from first principles. The programme is:

$$\underset{y^i, e^i, z^i}{\text{Max}} \ [p^iy^i - we^i - vz^i \mid y^i = F^i(e^i, z^i)], \quad (i = 1, 2)$$

or equivalently (dropping sector superscripts for clarity):

$$\underset{y, e, z}{\text{Max}} \ [pF(e, z) - we - vz].$$

The first order conditions are:

$$pF_e(e, z) - w = 0 \tag{2.56}$$

$$pF_z(e.z) - v = 0 \tag{2.57}$$

Now optimal factor demands will be functions of the exogenous parameters p, w, v. Hence we may write:

$$pF_e(e(p, w, v), z(p, w, v)) - w = 0 \tag{2.56'}$$

$$pF_z(e(p, w, v), z(p, w, v)) - v = 0 \tag{2.57'}$$

Differentiating $(2.56')$ with respect to v and $(2.57')$ with respect to w:

$$pF_{ee}e_v + pF_{ez}z_v = 0 \tag{2.58}$$

$$pF_{ze}e_w + pF_{zz}z_w = 0 \tag{2.59}$$

Hence:

$$F_{ee}e_v + F_{ez}z_v = 0 \qquad (2.60)$$

$$F_{ze}e_w + F_{zz}z_w = 0 \qquad (2.61)$$

Now:

$$(F_{ee}, z_v) \ll 0$$

by concavity of the production function and convexity of the profit function. Hence, by (2.60):

$$\text{sgn } F_{ez} = -\text{sgn } e_v$$

Similarly, by (2.61):

$$\text{sgn } F_{ze} = -\text{sgn } z_w.$$

Of course,

$$e_v^i = -\pi_{wv}^i = -\pi_{vw}^i = z_w^i$$

so,

$$\text{sgn } \pi_{wv}^i = \text{sgn } F_{ez}.$$

Let $F_{ez} > 0$ (i.e. an increase in one input will increase the marginal product of the other), then $\pi_{wv}^i > 0$.

We may therefore write:

$$y^i = \pi_i^i(p^i, w, v) \qquad (2.62)$$
$$ + \ \ - \ \ -$$

$$e^i = -\pi_w^i(p^i, w, v) \qquad (2.63)$$
$$ - \ \ + \ \ +$$

$$z^i = -\pi_v^i(p^i, w, v) \qquad (2.64)$$
$$ - \ \ + \ \ +$$

Proceeding as before, we can easily derive an equation analogous to (2.21) from the set of budget constraints:

$$p^1(y^1 - x^1 - g^1) + p^2(y^2 - x^2 - g^2) - v(z^1 + z^2)$$
$$+ (\Delta m^g - \Delta m^h - \Delta m^f)$$
$$+ w(\ell - e^1 - e^2) = 0 \qquad (2.65)$$

The model may again be reduced to the monetary approach by assuming instantaneous clearing of labour and non-tradeables markets.

$$p^2(y^2 - x^2 - g^2) - v(z^1 + z^2)$$
$$= \Delta m^h + \Delta m^f - (p^1 g^1 + p^2 g^2 - t) \qquad (2.66)$$

The LHS of (2.66) is of course the balance of trade surplus in terms of domestic currency. Equation (2.66) is thus the analogue of (2.25), i.e. it is the fundamental MABP equation with tradeables, non-tradeables and imported intermediate goods.

Rationing with Fixed Exchange Rates

Firms are the only agents whose behaviour alters as a result of allowing imported intermediate goods. In what follows it is important to bear in mind our assumption that tradeables' producers enjoy full priority in any implicit rationing scheme that may apply in the labour market.

Consider first the case of excess demand for labour, so that non-tradeables' producers are rationed in the labour market. We define the concept of the restricted profit function $\tilde{\pi}^1(\bar{e}; p^1, v)$:

$$\tilde{\pi}^1(\bar{e}; p^1, v) = \underset{e^1 z^1}{\text{Max}} \, [p^1 F^1(e^1, z^1) - we^1 - vz^1 | e^1$$
$$= \bar{\ell} + \pi_w^2(p^2, w, v) = \bar{e}]$$

where $\bar{\ell}$ is household labour supply. By applying the envelope theorem, it is clear that the normal derivative properties of the profit function hold, and in particular the restricted derived demand for oil, $\tilde{z}^1$ is:

$$\tilde{z}^1 = -\tilde{\pi}_v^1(\bar{e}, p^1, v).$$

Similarly, output supply is:

$$\tilde{y}^1 = \tilde{\pi}_1^1(\bar{e}, p^1, v).$$

Hence we may write the non-traded equilibrium locus under excess demand for labour (NTEL (EDL)):

$$\tilde{\pi}_1^1(\bar{e}, p^1, v) - x^1(p^1, p^2, w, \Omega) - g^1 = 0.$$

Now consider the behaviour of non-tradeables' producers under conditions of excess supply in the market for non-tradeables. Since firms in sector 1 are now subject to a demand constraint, the appropriate tool to use is thus the dual of the profit function, i.e. the cost function:

$$C^1(w, v, \bar{y}^1) = \underset{e^1, z^1}{\text{Min}} \quad [we^1 + vz^1 \mid F^1(e^1, z^1) = \bar{y}^1]$$

This will have the usual properties, viz: increasing in w and v, linear homogeneous and concave in w and v.

By an application of the envelope theorem we derive Shephard's Lemma:

$$e^1(w, v, \bar{y}) = C_w^1(w, v, \bar{y})$$

and

$$z^1(w, v, \bar{y}) = C_v^1(w, v, \bar{y}).$$

By the concavity of the cost function, the factor demands will have the correct slopes, i.e.:

$$(C_{ww}^1, C_{vv}^1) \ll 0.$$

If the constraint on output is binding, we must have:

$$F^1(e^1, z^1) = \bar{y}^1 \tag{2.67}$$

which is indeed one of the first-order conditions for cost minimization.

Differentiating (2.67) with respect to w and then with respect to v:

$$F^1_e e^1_w + F^1_z z^1_w = 0 \tag{2.68}$$

$$F^1_e e^1_v + F^1_z Z^1_v = 0. \tag{2.69}$$

But

$$(F^1_e, F^1_z) \gg 0; \quad (e^1_w, z^1_v) \ll 0 \tag{2.70}$$

Hence, $(z^1_w, e^1_v) \gg 0$

and we may write the conditional factor demands in the non-tradeables sector under conditions of excess supply of non-tradeables:

$$e^1 = C^1_w(w, v, \bar{y})$$
$$\quad\;\; - \; + \; +$$

$$z^1 = C^1_v(w, v, y).$$
$$\quad\;\; + \; - \; +$$

The labour market equilibrium locus under conditions of excess supply of the non-tradeable will therefore be (LMEL (ESNT)):

$$C^1_w - \pi^2_w - \ell = 0.$$

The labour market equilibrium locus under excess demand for non-tradeables (LMEL (EDNT)) and the non-tradeables' equilibrium locus under excess supply of labour (NTEL (ESL)) will be direct analogues of equations (2.43) and (2.41).

We can now gather together the various equilibrium loci for reference:

NTEL (ESL)
$$g^1 + \tilde{x}^1(\bar{\ell}, p^1, p^2, w, \Omega) - \pi_1^1(p^1, w, v) = 0 \qquad (2.71)$$

NTEL (EDL)
$$\tilde{\pi}_1^1(\bar{e}, p^1, v) - x^1(p^1, p^2, w, \Omega) - g^1 = 0 \qquad (2.72)$$

LMEL (ESNT)
$$C_w^1(w, v, \bar{y}^1) - \pi_w^2(p^2, w, v) - \ell(p^1, p^2, w, \Omega) = 0 \quad (2.73)$$

LMEL (EDNT)
$$\tilde{\ell}(\bar{x}^1, p^1, p^2, w, \Omega) + \pi_w^1(p^1, w, v)$$
$$+ \pi_w^2(p^1, w, v) = 0 \qquad (2.74)$$

where in (2.71): $\bar{\ell} = -\pi_w^1(p^1, w, v) - \pi_w^2(p^2, w, v)$

in (2.72): $\bar{e} = \ell(p^1, p^2, w) + \pi_w^2(p^2, w, v)$

in (2.73): $\bar{y}^1 = x^1(p^1, p^2, w, \Omega)$

and   in (2.74): $\bar{x}^1 = \pi_1^1(p^1, w, v)$.

Now the slope of (2.71) in (w, p^1) space will be given by an expression directly analogous to (2.41) and will be ambiguously signed, as discussed above. Similarly, for reasons discussed above, (2.74) will be positively signed, its slope being given by an expression analogous to (2.43).

Totally differentiating (2.72), allowing only w and p^1 to vary, and rearranging, we can show:

$$\frac{dw}{dp^1} \bigg|_{\substack{\text{NTE} \\ \text{EDL}}} = \frac{x_1^1 - \tilde{\pi}_{11}^1 - \tilde{\pi}_{1e}^1 \ell_1}{-x_w^1 + \pi_{1e}^1(\ell_w + \pi_{ww}^2)} \qquad (2.75)$$

Even if we make the reasonable assumption that $\tilde{\pi}_{1e} > 0$, the denominator of (2.75) is ambiguously signed; it captures the idea that an increase in wages will increase product demand but, by increasing labour supply and reducing the demand for labour in sector 2 and thereby relaxing a little the labour constraint on sector 1, it will lead to increased output of non-tradeables. If

$$\tilde{\pi}^1_{1e}(\ell_w + \pi^2_{ww}) > x^1_w$$

then raising wages leads to excess supply in the goods market. Similarly, in the numerator we see that an increase in price will reduce non-tradeables demand and increase output but will also reduce labour supply, further constraining non-tradeables' production. Clearly, then, the sign of (2.75) and hence the slope of (2.72) in (w, p^1) space are ambiguous. Similarly, from (2.73) it is easily shown:

$$\frac{dw}{dp^1}\bigg|_{\substack{LME \\ ESNT}} = \frac{\ell_1 - C^1_{wy}x_1}{C^1_{ww} - \pi^2_{ww} - \ell_1 + C^1_{wy}x^1_w} \qquad (2.76)$$

The numerator of (2.76) shows that increasing the price of non-tradeables will reduce labour supply but by reducing output demand will further constrain producers on the goods markets and so reduce labour demand. If

$$-C^1_{wy}x_1 > -\ell_1$$

then raising the price of non-tradeables will lead to excess supply in the labour market. Similarly, the first three terms in the denominator show that increasing the wage level will generally tend to produce excess supply of labour but the fourth term shows that by leading to a relaxation of the output constraint on producers a wage increase may in fact lead to excess demand. The slope of (2.73) in (w, p^1) space is thus ambiguous.

Collecting our observations enables us to draw Figure 2.11, which reflects the ambiguous slopes of three of the four sections of the equilibrium loci.

*Figure 2.11   Ambiguity in the slopes of the
               equilibrium loci*

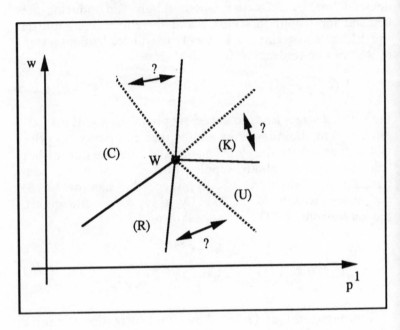

The ambiguity of the slopes of the loci (apart from NTEL (ESL)) is a direct consequence of introducing intermediate goods into the analysis. Another interesting result of having intermediate goods is the possibility of underconsumption ((2.72) and (2.73) are distinct), even when we allow tradeables' producers to enjoy full priority in the labour market — non-tradeables' producers can be simultaneously rationed in both the goods and the labour markets, owing to the non-invertibility of the production function which follows from allowing producers an extra degree of freedom in the form of intermediate inputs. This is similar to Muellbauer's and Portes's result that underconsumption is possible in a one-good model when firms are allowed to carry inventories (Muellbauer and Portes, 1978).

Effects of an Oil Price Shock

Malinvaud (1977) and Dixit (1978) analyse the effects of an oil price shock in fix-price models by asserting that a rise in the price of oil will have qualitatively similar results to a downward shift in productivity. Malinvaud (1977, pp. 90–1) thus posits that an oil price shock would shift the economy into classical unemployment. This assertion is echoed by Dixit (1978, p. 403). In the present model the effect of such a price rise may be analysed directly. However, whether or not the effect is ambiguous turns out to depend crucially on an earlier assumption.

Consider, for example, the NTEL (ESL) relation (2.71). An increase in v will reduce the supply of non-tradeables $(\pi^1_{1_v} < 0)$ which on its own would lead to a rightward shift of NTEL (ESL) (the region of excess demand for non-tradeables expands). However, since we assumed $F^i_{ez} > 0$, we have $e^i_v < 0$, so that an increase in oil price will contract labour demand and reduce the labour ration and hence demand for good.

The net effect will thus be ambiguous. In fact, it is easy to see that a rise in v will have an ambiguous effect on each of the four equilibrium loci, so that, starting from a point of Walrasian equilibrium, an oil shock can shift the economy into any of the four disequilibrium regimes.

If we assume $F^i_{ez} < 0$, then (2.71) shifts unambiguously to the right following an oil price rise. In fact, if we retain this assumption, then it follows straightforwardly that a rise in v* will reduce a rightward shift of NTEL (ESL), a rightward shift of NTEL (EDL), and a leftward shift of LMEL (ESNT) and LMEL (EDNT). Thus the region of repressed inflation expands and the region of Keynesian unemployment contracts, with relevant consequences for the other two regions. Thus, starting from an initial position of Walrasian equilibrium, a rise in the price of oil will shift the economy into a state of repressed inflation (Figure 2.12), in contrast to the intuitive arguments of Malinvaud and Dixit but only at the expense of assuming $F_{ez} < 0$. Otherwise the effect is ambiguous. Although the theory of the firm has nothing

Figure 2.12   Effects of an oil price shock

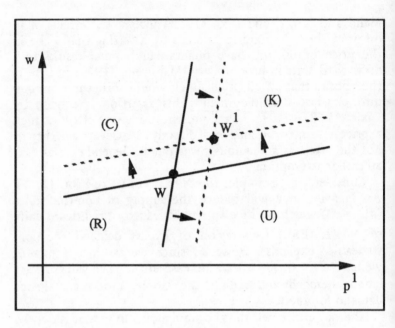

to say on the sign of F_{ez}, it is probably true that most economists would sign it as positive (see Henderson and Quandt, 1980, p. 81).

If we assume that labour is supplied inelastically, then we can get slightly sharper conclusions. Consider LMEL (EDNT) (2.74). An increase in v* and hence v contracts the demand for labour. Although the non-tradeable ration will also contract, this will have no feedback effect on effective labour supply, by the inelasticity assumption. The net effect will thus be a downward shift of LMEL (EDNT). This implies that the new equilibrium will be due south of the old one — or that the economy must move from Walrasian equilibrium into either Keynesian or classical unemployment. Moreover, if labour supply is assumed to be highly but not perfectly inelastic, this result would still be likely to follow. This accords broadly with the experience of the Western nations since 1973.

CONCLUSION

In this chapter we have analysed a fix-price general equilibrium model of a small open economy with tradeables and non-tradeables and also with an imported intermediate good. We found that when the real side was assumed to clear continuously, the predictions of both models were fully consistent with those of the monetary approach to the balance of payments. In particular, both a devaluation and a pure increase in the money supply were long-run neutral. However, the crucial assumption in the Walrasian model was that the real side of the economy cleared continuously *ex ante*, and it is hard to see how this can occur without swift adjustment of prices. We therefore find it difficult to justify the claim of Frenkel and Johnson:

> The monetary approach to the balance of payments . . . can be readily applied to conditions of price and wage rigidity and consequent response of quantities — unemployment, output, consumption — rather than money wages and prices to monetary changes (1976a, p. 25).

In temporary equilibrium with Keynesian unemployment we derived a six elasticities condition for a devaluation to improve the trade balance. In the Mark I model we also indicated that an increase in the real wage may not lead exclusively to classical unemployment.

When an imported intermediate good was introduced into the analysis, the ambiguities were multiplied. In particular, we showed that an oil price rise may send the economy from a point of Walrasian equilibrium into any of the four disequilibrium regimes, although either Keynesian or classical unemployment was more likely to result the more inelastic was labour supply. The models of Malinvaud (1977), Dixit (1978), Neary (1980) and Steigum (1980) are each increasingly more general in terms of considering traded goods, non-tradeables and imported intermediate goods. The cost of increasing this generality has been to reduce the sharpness of the model's predictions. In the section 'The Mark II Model' (pp. 72–82) we showed that these models have in some ways only avoided total ambiguity by precluding certain general equilibrium effects.

However, the fact remains that an oil price shock will shift the economy from Walrasian equilibrium into one of the four disequilibrium regimes — probably Keynesian or classical unemployment. At least one explanation of the underlying causes of the world recession during the 1970s would be that such disequilibrium behaviour was triggered by the first oil shock of 1973. This suggests that even if the monetary approach is applicable at an aggregate level to the period of the 1960s (there was after all virtually full employment and very low inflation), an analysis of the ensuing period cannot avoid an explicit analysis of the real side. Errors of generalization such as the following might then be avoided:

> More fundamentally, the assumption of normally full employment reflects the passage of time and the accumulation of experience of reasonably full employment as the historical norm rather than the historical rarity that Keynes's theory and left-wing Keynesian mythology made it out to be (Frenkel and Johnson, 1976a, p. 25).

APPENDIX 2.1: INTERTEMPORAL PROGRAMMING, EXPECTATIONS AND MONEY BALANCES

In the text we assumed a (reduced-to-one period) utility function of the form:

$$u = u(x, H-\ell, m) \tag{A2.1}$$

where x is the amount of good consumed in the current period (we abstract from the tradeables/non-tradeables distinction here) and H, ℓ and m are fixed labour endowment, labour supply and nominal money balances respectively. A more usual method would be to use the argument m/p_0, where p_0 is an index of the expected future price level. Since the expected future price level, wages, etc. depend on the current ones, all elasticities must be understood to include the effects arising through expectations. More rigorously, if $_ix$, $_i\ell$, $_ip$, $_i\pi$ and $_iw$ are expectations or plans on the appropriate variables i periods in the future, then we might specify the consumer's utility function as:

$$u = u(x, {}_ix, \ldots, {}_hx, H-\ell, H-{}_i\ell, \ldots, H-{}_h\ell, {}_hm)$$

where h is the consumer's time horizon and $_hm$ is a bequest at the end of period h. The household will maximize u subject to:

$$px + \sum_{i=1}^{h} {}_1p_1x + {}_hm = w\ell + \sum_{i=1}^{h} w_i\ell + \sum_{i=1}^{h} ({}_i\pi - t) + \Omega$$

Now Benassy (1975, p. 516) has shown that this problem is equivalent to maximizing a utility function of the form (A2.1), subject to the current-period budget constraint. It is important to realize, however, that the reduced-to-one period utility function depends upon anticipated prices and constraints, and thus upon today's perceived constraints.

In order to highlight some of the problems in deriving a demand for money balances, and especially a demand for real balances, consider the following schematic analysis.

Without loss of generality consider a consumer facing a

two-period utility maximization problem. Assume that there are two goods vectors, distinguishable only by their temporal context, x^1 and x^2 available in periods one and two respectively. Let the spot price vector p^1 and current disposable income (including initial endowments) be y^1. Let p^2 and y^2 be corresponding expected discounted values for period 2.

We assume consumers have point expectations held with certainty and y^2 is linear homogeneous in p^2. Again without loss of generality, we assume labour is supplied inelastically.

Let the consumer's utility function take the simplistic form: $u(x^1, x^2)$. Then its maximization programme is:

$$\underset{x^1,\, x^2}{\text{Max}}\; [u(x^1, x^2) \mid p^1 . x^1 + p^2 . x^2 = y^1 + y^2(p^2)].$$
$$(A2.2)$$

The dual to (A2.2) is:

$$\underset{x^1,\, x^2}{\text{Min}}\; [p^1 . x^1 + p^2 . x^2 \mid u(x^1, x^2) = \bar{u}] \qquad (A2.3)$$

where $\bar{u}$ is the solution to (A2.2).

(A2.3) yields the expenditure function:

$\epsilon(p^1, p^2, \bar{u})$, which may be set equal to income:

$$\epsilon(p^1, p^2, \bar{u}) = y^1 + y^2(p^2) \qquad (A2.4)$$

Now write:

$$E(p^1, p^2, \bar{u}) = \epsilon(p^1, p^2, \bar{u}) - y^2(p^2) = y^1 \qquad (A2.5)$$

Now, by the envelope theorem:

$$\frac{\partial E}{\partial p^1} = \frac{\partial \epsilon}{\partial p^1} = x^1 \qquad (A2.6)$$

$$\frac{\partial E}{\partial p^2} = \frac{\partial \epsilon}{\partial p^2} - \frac{\partial y^2}{\partial p^2} \qquad (A2.7)$$

Now y^2 is expected income in period 2 and if we assume

that consumer expectations are consistent, since period 2 is the last period y^2 will be equal to profit in period 2:

$$y^2 = \pi^2(.) \tag{A2.8}$$

Now, by the envelope theorem:

$$\frac{\partial \pi^2}{\partial p^2} = \frac{\partial y^2}{\partial p^2} = \sigma^2 \tag{A2.9}$$

where σ^2 is supply in period 2; whilst

$$\frac{\partial \epsilon}{\partial p^2} = x^2 \tag{A2.10}$$

So, from (A2.9) and (A2.10) we see that (A2.7) is the excess demand function in period 2. Further, since $\epsilon(.)$ is linear homogeneous in prices, so will $E(.)$ be, thus:

$$\frac{\partial E}{\partial p^1} \cdot p^1 + \frac{\partial E}{\partial p^2} \cdot p^2 = E \tag{A2.11}$$

and $\dfrac{\partial E}{\partial p^2} \cdot p^2 = y^1 - p^1 . x^1$

So $\dfrac{\partial E}{\partial p^2} \cdot p^2$ is the amount of money carried forward to the next period and the plans become consistent. Thus, $\dfrac{\partial E}{\partial p^2} \cdot p^2$ is the demand for nominal balances. Whether or not we can decompose this into a demand for and 'price' of real balances depends upon whether this dot product can be decomposed. In particular we must be able to write $E(.)$ as a function of p^1, u and some scalar aggregate of the expected price vector p^2. Say this is possible, and call the appropriate scalar-valued mapping $\kappa(p^2)$, which we assume homogeneous in p^2. Then we can write:

$$\frac{\partial E}{\partial p^2} \cdot p^2 = \frac{\partial E}{\partial \kappa} \cdot \frac{\partial \kappa}{\partial p^2} \cdot p^2$$

$$= \frac{\partial E}{\partial \kappa} \cdot \kappa(p^2)$$

Thus, $\kappa(p^2)$ can be thought of as the price and $\frac{\partial E}{\partial \kappa}$ the demand for real balances.

The conditions under which the vector p^2 can be aggregated in the expenditure function are given by the Leontief Aggregation Theorem (Leontief, 1947), which in this context demands that the ratio of planned excess demands for any pair of goods in the future must be independent of spot prices and of the level of utility. Note that with only one good in each period the conditions are satisfied trivially. In the more general context the conditions become extremely restrictive, however, especially when considered in conjunction with the assumption of point expectations held with certainty. However, in order to conform with previous practice, this chapter implicitly assumes that the aggregate condition is satisfied.

Other attempts at modelling expectations in a disequilibrium context include Dixit, 1976; Muellbauer and Portes, 1978; and Neary and Stiglitz, 1982.

3. Empirical Models of the Monetary Approach: A Critique

INTRODUCTION

As we pointed out in Chapter 1, the MABP has enjoyed a fairly high degree of success empirically; for surveys see Magee (1976) and Kreinin and Officer (1978). The purpose of this chapter is to examine critically some of the evidence that has been adduced in connection with the MABP. In section 1 we give an exposition of the derivation of the empirical model which has often been used to test the MABP in the literature. Section 2 examines the question of the exogeneity specification of the standard empirical model, whilst section 3 looks at the potentially more serious implications of the use of identities in the modelling process. The main points made in the chapter are, firstly, that Granger-type tests of causality should not be used to detect simultaneous sterilization or to suggest appropriate estimators; and secondly, that many empirical studies of the monetary approach to the balance of payments can be shown to be little more than the reproduction of a money stock identity in disguise.

AN EMPIRICAL MODEL OF THE MABP

Empirical specifications of the MABP generally take as their starting point the balance sheet of the monetary authorities (that is the central bank and exchange-stabilization authorities combined), represented here as Table 3.1, where:

R = official holdings of international reserves;

OA = all other assets of the monetary authorities;
H = stock of high-powered money;
OL = all other liabilities of the monetary authorities.

Table 3.1 Monetary authorities' balance sheet

Assets	Liabilities
R	H
OA	OL

High-powered money is defined:

$$H \equiv R + (OA - OL) = R + D \tag{3.1}$$

where D = stock of domestic credit made available by the monetary authorities.

Now if M_s be the stock supply of domestic money:

$$M_s \equiv kH \tag{3.2}$$

where k is the money multiplier, from (3.1) and (3.2):

$$M_s \equiv k(R + D) \tag{3.3}$$

Now assume a stable demand for money function:

$$M_d = L(p, y, r); \tag{3.4}$$

$$L_p > 0; L_y > 0; L_r < 0;$$

$$\eta_p > 0; \eta_y > 0; \eta_r < 0$$

where the L_i's denote partial derivatives and the η_i's elasticities and:

p = domestic price level;
y = domestic real income;

r = interest rate.

Assuming constant elasticities we can write more specifically:

$$\ln M_d = \ln C + \eta_p \ln p + \eta_y \ln y + \eta_r \ln r \qquad (3.5)$$

where C is a scale factor.

From (3.3) and (3.5) the money market equilibrium condition is:

$$\ln k + \ln(R+D) = \ln C + \eta_p \ln p + \eta_y \ln y + \eta_r \ln r \qquad (3.6)$$

Differentiating and rearranging:

$$\frac{dR}{R+D} = \eta_p d\ln p + \eta_y d\ln y + \eta_r d\ln r - d\ln k - \frac{dD}{R+D} \qquad (3.7)$$

Or, approximating the differential operator by the first difference operator:

$$\frac{\Delta R}{R+D} = \eta_p \Delta \ln p + \eta_p \Delta \ln y + \eta_r \Delta \ln r - \Delta \ln k - \frac{\Delta D}{R+D} \qquad (3.8)$$

Equation (3.8) is comparable to the model discussed in Johnson (1972). It has generally been turned into an empirical model by tacking on an error term satisfying the classical assumptions. The model is then estimated directly as:

$$\frac{\Delta R}{R+D} = a_0 + a_1 \Delta \ln p + a_2 \Delta \ln y + a_3 \Delta \ln r$$
$$+ a_4 \Delta \ln k + a_5 \frac{\Delta D}{R+D} + u \qquad (3.9)$$

Support or otherwise for the MABP is then adduced according to how far the parameter estimates conform to the MABP priors which we infer by comparing (3.8) with (3.9):

$$a_0 = 0; a_1 = 1; a_2 > 0; a_3 < 0; a_4 = -1; a_5 = -1 \qquad (3.10)$$

The restrictions (3.10) are thus taken as a joint null hypothesis that the MABP is a valid description of real-world processes. For examples of studies which use this framework or some variant of it, see, *inter alia*, Bean, 1976; Genberg, 1976; Zecher, 1976; Aghelvi and Khan, 1977; Akhtar, Putnam and Wilford, 1977; Cox and Wilford, 1977; and Putnam and Wilford, 1977.

Relation (3.3) is generally referred to as the monetary base identity and equation (3.9) as the standard reserve-flow equation (Kreinin and Officer, 1978). The coefficient on ($\Delta D/H$) is referred to as the offset coefficient, and is purported to show the degree to which changes in the domestic component of the monetary base are offset by changes in the international component of the high-powered stock. As we have pointed out, the MABP theory suggests that under a fixed-rate regime the value of the offset coefficient is minus unity, implying that monetary policy is completely neutralized by the balance of payments.

The question naturally arises as to whether the restrictions (3.10) uniquely identify a data-generating process corresponding to the monetary approach or whether they may be implied by some other theory, i.e. is there a problem of observational equivalence?

A standard Keynesian analysis of the effect of a rise in domestic credit might run as follows. An increase in the domestic component of the monetary base is multiplied up to an increase in the domestic money supply. This increases the (demand-determined) equilibrium level of real income and drives down interest rates (the LM curve shifts to the right). A marginal propensity to import lying in the open interval (0, 1) then implies a deterioration on current account, whilst the fall in interest rates leads to a deterioration on capital account. The net outcome is a deterioration of the balance of payments where the values of the relevant propensities and elasticities are such that an initial increase in the monetary base is only partly counteracted by a reserve outflow, thus retaining a net positive change in the monetary base and hence in the money supply. In terms of the above empirical model this translates into the offset coefficient lying in the open interval (−1, 0). It is thus the nearness of the offset coefficient to minus unity rather than its negativity which provides a test of the MABP against non-monetary alternatives. A traditional Mundellian 'policy mix' model would, however, reverse the signs of the coefficients on interest rate growth and real income growth (recall Table 1.1).

2 EXOGENEITY AND THE MABP: WHAT DO GRANGER TESTS SHOW?

The interpretation of empirical tests of the MABP is complicated by the controversy concerning the exogeneity specification implicit in the empirical model. In particular, if the authorities attempt to sterilize reserve inflows by adjusting the level of domestic credit, ordinary least squares estimates of the standard reserve-flow equation may be biased and inconsistent. Recently, attempts have been made to resolve the controversy by applying Granger-type causality tests to the data (Blejer, 1979; Johannes, 1981). Sub-section 2.1 discusses the general problem of exogeneity in the MABP empirical model and sub-section 2.2 introduces a test based on Granger's (1969) definition of causality. Results for UK data are then reported. Sub-section 2.4 then discusses further the relationship between Granger-type tests and weak exogeneity.

The Problem, and a Proposed Test

Specifically, the empirical model of the MABP assumes the exogeneity with respect to reserve flows of real national income, the price level, interest rates, the money multiplier and the level of domestic credit. This assumption is highlighted by the claim of many MABP advocates that equation (3.1) is a reduced form (see for example, Whitman, 1975; Aghelvi and Khan, 1977; and Swoboda, 1977).

If these assumptions are in fact incorrect, then, as Geweke (1978) notes, there are three main implications. Firstly,

standard estimators will be inconsistent; secondly, structural
equations may be unidentified (e.g. Argy and Kouri, 1974);
and, thirdly, the standard equation may be a misspecification
of the dynamics of the true model.

Reasons for suspecting endogeneity of certain variables are
far from arcane. As Magee (1976) points out, for example, an
autonomous increase in reserves which thereby raises the
domestic money supply might be expected to raise the level
of income and prices and to depress interest rates. Such
mechanisms would imply an upward bias in the OLS
estimates of the appropriate coefficients.

Perhaps the most controversial issue in this area is the
presence or otherwise of sterilization: the authorities may
wish to offset the effects of reserve flows on the domestic
economy by deliberately adjusting the level of domestic
credit. Johnson writes:

> The new approach assumes − in some cases, asserts − that these
> monetary inflows or outflows associated with surpluses or deficits
> are not sterilised − or cannot be, within a period relevant to policy
> analysis − but instead influence the domestic money supply
> (Johnson, 1976, p. 152).

Say there is an exogenous increase in money demand.
Without an accommodating increase in domestic credit there
will be, *ex hypothesi*, an inflow of reserves to meet this
demand. If the government *partially* offsets this inflow,
reducing domestic credit by some fraction S, say, then
domestic money demand will be unsatisfied by this amount.
As reserves commensurate with this amount flow in in the
second round, the government reduces domestic credit by
a fraction S, or a fraction S^2 of the original level. And so the
process continues. This will lead to biased OLS estimates of
the coefficient of the domestic credit variable:

$$|\hat{a}_5| = 1/(1-S).$$

In the UK, this process may in the past have operated
almost automatically in the following way: an overall BOP
deficit (reserve loss) involves intervention by the authorities

in the foreign exchange market to defend sterling. Thus, more sterling accrues to the Exchange Equalisation Account, which immediately purchases Treasury Bills. Thus, an increase in domestic deficit leads to an increase in domestic credit expansion, rather than a fall in the growth of the money supply.

All of the issues raised in this section so far imply that a formal testing of the exogeneity specification is in order. One way of doing this is by adopting the Wiener–Granger notion of exogeneity or causality (see Granger, 1969; Sims, 1972; Enoch, 1979). Blejer (1979) has tested the exogeneity of domestic credit with respect to reserves in several European countries using the bivariate methods proposed by Sims (1972). However, such bivariate tests ignore the potential impact of other variables typically associated with the MABP (the potential effects of this are well documented by Skoog, 1976). In this sense the tests in this section, being systems tests, are closer in nature to those of Johannes (1981).

The Tests

The exogeneity tests in this section are based on the work of Geweke (1978) and to a certain extent follow the analysis of Johannes (1981). Consider the complete dynamic simultaneous equations model (CDSEM) (Geweke 1978):

$$B(L)y_t + \Gamma(L)x_t = \epsilon_t \qquad (3.11)$$
$$(gxg)(gx1) \quad (gxk)(kx1) \quad (gx1)$$

where $E(\epsilon_t) = 0, \forall t;$

$COV(\epsilon_t, x_{t-s}) = 0, \quad \forall t, \forall s > 0;$

$COV(\epsilon_t, y_{t-s}) = 0, \quad \forall t, \forall s > 0.$

$B(L)$ and $\Gamma(L)$ are matrices of polynomials of infinite order in non-negative powers of the lag operator L, with the roots of $B(L)$ outside the unit circle. The CDSEM purports to be a complete description of the interactions between k putative exogenous variables x_t and g endogenous variables y_t.

Geweke draws two implications with respect to the CDSEM. Firstly, since current and past elements of x_t are inputs while y_t is output, only past and current (and not future) values of x_t affect y_t in the CDSEM. This has been noted by engineers (Caines and Chan, 1975) and was introduced into the economic literature by Sims (1972). Secondly, since, *ex hypothesi*, x_t is determined outside of the CDSEM, 'a proper specification of the determination of x_t will not include any values of y_t' (1978, p. 166).

Thus, in the regression of x_t as in infinite-order ARDL on itself and y_t, viz:

$$x_t = \sum_1^\infty F_s x_{t-s} + \sum_1^\infty G_s y_{t-s} + \epsilon_t \qquad (3.12)$$

there 'exists a CDSEM with exogenous x_t and endogenous y_t, and no other variables, if and only if $G_s = 0$, $\forall s > 0$' (Dent and Geweke, 1979). In these terms, then, exogeneity in the sense we have outlined appears to become an empirically testable hypothesis via the finite parameterization of (3.12).

In implementing this finite parameterization, as Geweke (1978) points out, we have to reconcile the criteria of test unbiasedness which demands a generous parameterization, and power, which automatically diminishes as the parameter space is expanded. Considering the seasonal dynamics of quarterly data and the available degrees of freedom, we chose to include four lags on both the putative endogenous variable (i.e. the reserve-flow variable) and on the putative exogenous variables.

Using this finite parameterization of (3.12) tests of the hypothesis:

$$H_0 : G_s = 0, \ \forall s > 0 \qquad (3.13)$$

were carried out on UK data for three periods: 1964 II–1979 III (whole sample period), 1964 II–1971 IV (fixed-rate period) and 1973 I–1979 III (floating-rate period). The data are described in section 3.1 below and sources are listed in Appendix 5.1.

The vector process (3.12) was estimated by individual ordinary least squares regressions; this is equivalent to full information maximum likelihood estimation to within a small error of approximation (and fully equivalent if the first observation is treated as non-stochastic). Tests of the null were carried out by Wald and likelihood ratio test procedures.

Since the restrictions (3.13) represent a set of *linear* restrictions expressable in the form: $R\beta = r$ (usual notation), the Wald test statistic takes the form:

$$W = \frac{(r-R\beta)' \left\{ R[X'(\Omega^{-1}\otimes I)X]^{-1} R' \right\}^{-1} (r-R\beta)(MT-m)}{(Y-X\beta)'(\Omega^{-1}\otimes I)(Y-X\beta)}$$

where M = number of equations;
   T = sample size;
   m = number of coefficients in the system;
   β = unrestricted coefficient estimates;
   Ω = estimated contemporaneous covariance matrix.

Under the null this is asymptotically distributed as $\chi^2(q)$, where q is the number of restrictions, and will tend to be large under the alternative ($H_1: R_\beta \neq r$); for a derivation of a corresponding F test (equal to W/q since $F(q, MT-m)$ converges asymptotically in distribution to $(1/q)\chi^2(q)$). See Theil (1971, pp. 313–14).

The second test we applied was a likelihood ratio test statistic of the form:

$$LR = T \cdot \ln (|\Omega_o| / |\Omega|)$$

where Ω_o and Ω are the estimated contemporaneous covariance matrices of the restricted and unrestricted systems respectively. Under the null this is asymptotically distributed as a central chi-square with degrees of freedom equal to the number of restrictions, q.

Table 3.2 Results of the systems Granger-causality tests

Period	Wald	Value	LR	Value	Regression	R^2	$\bar{R}^2$	F stat.		Value	Marginal significance
'64II–'79III	$\chi^2(20)$ =	34.468	$\chi^2(20)$	= 31.7744	Δlnp	0.68	0.63	$F(4, 38)$	=	0.5254	0.7177
	ms* =	0.0231	ms*	= 0.0458	Δlny	0.83	0.80	$F(4, 38)$	=	1.3110	0.2834
Whole Sample Period					Δlnr	0.19	0.07	$F(4, 38)$	=	0.2942	0.8800
					Δlnk	0.43	0.34	$F(4, 38)$	=	1.7440	0.1605
					$\Delta D/(R+D)$	0.40	0.31	$F(4, 38)$	=	4.5740	0.0041
'64II–'71IV	$\chi^2(20)$ =	56.93	$\chi^2(20)$	= 55.5541	Δlnp	0.56	0.40	$F(4, 7)$	=	1.3576	0.3389
	ms* =	0.00005	ms*	= 0.00003	Δlny	0.94	0.93	$F(4, 7)$	=	0.5450	0.7090
Fixed-Rate Period					Δlnr	0.17	-0.13	$F(4, 7)$	=	0.8228	0.5501
					Δlnk	0.71	0.61	$F(4, 7)$	=	3.9163	0.0560
					$\Delta D/(R+D)$	0.78	0.70	$F(4, 7)$	=	7.8590	0.0100
'73I–'79III	$\chi^2(20)$ =	15.794	$\chi^2(20)$	= 14.3564	Δlnp	0.55	0.35	$F(4, 3)$	=	0.3864	0.8096
	ms* =	0.7293	ms*	= 0.8120	Δlny	0.74	0.63	$F(4, 3)$	=	0.9041	0.5556
Floating-Rate Period					Δlnr	0.35	0.06	$F(4, 3)$	=	0.5656	0.7080
					Δlnk	0.51	0.29	$F(4, 3)$	=	0.2477	0.8945
					$\Delta D/(R+D)$	0.43	0.18	$F(4, 3)$	=	2.0212	0.2948

*'ms' denotes 'marginal significance' level.

Results

Results of the tests are reported in Table 3.2. As can be seen, the likelihood ratio and Wald tests are broadly consistent with one another for each period and, as we should expect, $W > LR$ (Berndt and Savin, 1979).

For the sample period as a whole we can reject the hypothesis of exogeneity at the 5 per cent level. Interestingly, exogeneity can be easily rejected for the fixed-rate sub-period at the 1 per cent level, whilst for the floating-rate sub-period exogeneity cannot be rejected at all at any reasonable level of significance.

More detailed regression results are also included in Table 3.2. These show results of the F-tests that the coefficients on the reserve-flow variables in each individual equation are zero. Although they do not take account of other variables in the system, they do shed some light as to which putative exogenous variables are causing the systems test to reject exogeneity of the entire set. The domestic credit variable appears to be the major culprit. For the period as a whole, the test statistic on domestic credit is significant at the 1 per cent level, whilst the nearest level of significance for other regressions over the period is 16 per cent. Similar considerations apply to the fixed-rate period, except that the statistic on the money-multiplier regression is significant at the 7 per cent level.

To sum up this section, if we accept the MABP on its own terms and limit the analysis to the fixed-rate period, then our results are in accordance with those of Johannes, and in direct contrast to those of Blejer, i.e. we reject the exogeneity specification of the MABP. Moreover, examination of the individual regression results provides strong support for the sterilization hypothesis. What does this imply for the econometrics of the monetary approach?

Causality and Exogeneity

The notion of causation has been a topic of considerable philosophical controversy at least since Hume (1776). In econometrics the problem has been raised in the context of the choice of exogenous variables in a regression model and dates at least from Frisch (1938). In general the approach has been to determine the causal ordering *a priori* by an appeal to economic theory and to regress the putative effect variable on the putative causal variables.

Despite important early contributions by, *inter alios*, the Cowles Foundation economists (Koopmans and Hood, 1953; Koopmans, 1950), the direction of causality was thought of for many years an inherently non-testable, *a priori* proposition. Using methods developed originally by engineers (Caines and Chan, 1975; Wiener, 1956), Granger (1969) and Sims (1972) introduced a notion of causation into the econometric literature which appeared to have testable implications. The basic intuition behind the Wiener–Granger notion of causation is that x is said to (Granger) cause y if a better prediction of y can be made by including the past history of x in the conditioned information set of the prediction. Sims and others have asserted that Granger-type causality tests may be used to yield evidence on the appropriate direction of regression (Sims, 1972, p. 550).

Hitherto, causality tests have mainly been used in macroeconomics and in particular to test monetarist versus Keynesian assumptions about the causal ordering between the money supply and income. More recently they have been used in conjunction with rational expectations hypothesis testing (see, for example, Spreen and Shankwiler, 1979).

Unfortunately, various studies using similar test procedures have produced contradictory evidence concerning the relationship between money and income (for a survey see Slough, 1981). Moreover, Monte Carlo evidence suggests the existence of substantial differences in power between various causality tests and that one could easily produce conflicting conclusions by employing a battery of causality tests on the same data sets (see Belsen and Schwert, 1981; Geweke, Meese and Dent, 1983) — a conclusion that would probably come as no surprise to many applied econometricians (see Leamer, 1978).

In our analysis of this problem, applied to empirical models of the monetary approach, we assume that there exists in reality a *data-generating structure* which consists of a set of simultaneous behavioural equations whose stochastic structure is encapsulated in a set of well behaved error terms. Solving the system for the variables of interest then gives a reduced form in terms of other (non-stochastic) variables and disturbance terms. The variables of interest will then have a joint (normal) distribution with given mean and covariance matrix. An ordinary least squares regression of one variable on another can then be interpreted in terms of the conditional regression model, but now we can give a meaning to the resulting estimators being biased in comparison with the parameters of the structural form. By using a collapsed form of the standard reserve-flow equation, we then show that the ordinary least squares estimator of the offset coefficient may be biased and inconsistent when sterilization but not Granger causality is present, and may be asymptotically unbiased when Granger causality runs from reserves to the domestic credit variable.

The static case

For ease of exposition, consider a collapsed form of the standard reserve-flow equation where an international reserves variable r_t (which may be the growth in the reserve component of the monetary base) is a linear function of a domestic credit variable d_t and one other variable m_t (e.g. money demand), together with a stochastic disturbance (equation (3.14)). Assume also that there exists a government sterilization function in which the domestic credit variable is a linear function of the international reserves variable and some other (identifying, non-stochastic) target variable x_t (equation (3.15)) plus a disturbance term (see, for example, Genberg, 1976):

$$r_t = ad_t + bm_t + u_t \tag{3.14}$$

$$d_t = \alpha r_t + \beta x_t + v_t \tag{3.15}$$

$$\begin{bmatrix} u_t \\ v_t \end{bmatrix} \sim \text{IN} \begin{bmatrix} 0, & \begin{vmatrix} \sigma_{11} & \sigma_{12} \\ \sigma_{12} & \sigma_{22} \end{vmatrix} \end{bmatrix}$$

The reduced form is:

$$r_t = \frac{a\beta}{1-aa} x_t + \frac{b}{1-aa} m_t + \eta_t$$

$$d_t = \frac{\beta}{1-aa} x_t + \frac{ab}{1-aa} m_t + \epsilon_t$$

where $\eta_t = \dfrac{u_t + av_t}{1-aa}$

and $\epsilon_t = \dfrac{au_t + v_t}{1-aa}$

Hence:

$$\begin{bmatrix} \eta_t \\ \epsilon_t \end{bmatrix} \sim IN \left[0, \begin{Bmatrix} \omega_{11} & \omega_{12} \\ \omega_{12} & \omega_{22} \end{Bmatrix} \right]$$

where:

$$\omega_{11} = \frac{a\,\sigma_{22} + \sigma_{11} + 2a\sigma_{12}}{(1-aa)^2}$$

$$\omega_{22} = \frac{\sigma_{22} + a^2\sigma_{11} + 2a\sigma_{12}}{(1-aa)^2}$$

$$\omega_{12} = \frac{a\sigma_{22} + a\sigma_{11} + (1+aa)\sigma_{12}}{(1-aa)^2}$$

The conditional expectation of r_t given d_t then suggests the regression:

$$r_t = Ax_t + Bm_t + Cd_t + \xi_t \tag{3.16}$$
$$\xi_t \sim N(0, \omega^2)$$

where:

$$A = \frac{-\beta(a\sigma_{11} + \sigma_{12})}{\sigma_{22} + a^2\sigma_{11} + 2a\sigma_{12}}$$

$$B = \frac{-b(\sigma_{22} + a\sigma_{12})}{\sigma_{22} + a^2\sigma_{11} + 2a\sigma_{12}}$$

$$C = \frac{a\sigma_{11} + a\sigma_{22} + (1+aa)\sigma_{12}}{a^2\sigma_{11} + \sigma_{22} + 2a\sigma_{12}}$$

$$\xi_t = r_t - E(r_t | d_t)$$

$$\omega^2 = \frac{\sigma_{11}\sigma_{22} - \sigma_{12}^2}{\sigma_{22} + a^2\sigma_{11} + 2a\sigma_{12}}$$

Comparing the conditional regression model (3.16) with the structural equation (3.14) we can see that in an ordinary least squares regression of r_t on d_t, x_t and m_t the crucial requirement for the least squares estimator of the coefficient on d_t to be a consistent estimator of the offset coefficient a is that $a = 0$ in (3.15) and $\sigma_{12} = 0$; i.e. that there is no (instantaneous) sterilization of reserve inflows and that the structure is well-defined in the sense that the errors are orthogonal. If both $a = 0$ and $\sigma_{12} = 0$, then the conditional regression model reduces to the structural reserve-flow equation (3.14). If $\sigma_{12} = 0$ but $a \neq 0$, then

$$C = \frac{a\sigma_{11} + a\sigma_{22}}{a^2\sigma_{11} + \sigma_{22}}$$

$$= a + \frac{a(1-aa)\sigma_{11}}{\sigma_{22} + a^2\sigma_{11}}$$

so that ordinary least squares estimation of (3.14) will yield a biased and inconsistent estimator of the offset coefficient.

Further, since we expect both a and a to lie in the closed interval [-1, 0], the bias will be negative and the OLS estimator of a will in general be biased upwards in absolute value. The important point to note, however, is that in the structural model (3.14), (3.15) r_t does not Granger-cause d_t — there is instantaneous bidirectional feedback. Nevertheless, (3.14) is not a reduced form and ordinary least squares estimators will be biased and inconsistent.

A dynamic reaction function

Now consider a truly dynamic reaction function through which the reserves variable does in fact Granger-cause the domestic credit variable. We retain the reserve-flow equation (3.14) but postulate that the authorities will set the domestic credit variable according to the level of both variables in the previous period (here and throughout we limit the depth of the lag structure to one period, since multiplying lags merely complicates the algebra without significantly altering the results). This makes intuitive sense, since the reserve-flow equation is presumably the outcome of maximizing behaviour, whilst the government reaction function may operate with lags, owing to informational problems. The true data-generating structure is then assumed to be of the form:

$$r_t = ad_t + bm_t + u_t \qquad (3.14)$$

$$d_t = \gamma d_{t-1} + \delta r_{t-1} + v_t \qquad (3.17)$$

$$\begin{bmatrix} u_t \\ v_t \end{bmatrix} \sim IN \left[0, \begin{Bmatrix} \sigma_{11} & \sigma_{12} \\ \sigma_{12} & \sigma_{22} \end{Bmatrix} \right]$$

The reduced form is:

$$r_t = a\gamma d_{t-1} + a\delta r_{t-1} + bm_t + \eta_t$$

$$d_t = \gamma d_{t-1} + \delta r_{t-1} + v_t$$

where $\eta_t = u_t + av_t$.

Hence:

$$\begin{bmatrix} \eta_t \\ v_t \end{bmatrix} \sim \text{IN} \begin{bmatrix} 0, & \begin{matrix} \omega_{11} & \omega_{12} \\ \omega_{12} & \omega_{22} \end{matrix} \end{bmatrix}$$

where:

$$\omega_{11} = \sigma_{11} + a^2\sigma_{22} + 2a\sigma_{12}$$

$$\omega_{22} = \sigma_{22}$$

$$\omega_{12} = \sigma_{12} + a\sigma_{22}$$

The conditional expectation of r_t given d_t now suggests the regression model:

$$r_t = Ad_t + Bm_t + Cd_{t-1} + Dr_{t-1} + \theta_t \qquad (3.18)$$

$$\theta_t \sim N(0, \rho^2)$$

where:

$$A = a + \sigma_{12}/\sigma_{22}$$
$$B = b$$
$$C = -\gamma\sigma_{12}/\sigma_{22}$$
$$D = -\delta\sigma_{12}/\sigma_{22}$$
$$\theta_t = r_t - E(r_t|d_t, r_{t-1})$$
$$\rho^2 = \sigma_{11} - \sigma_{12}^2/\sigma_{22}$$

Now if the error terms in the structural form are orthogonal so that $\sigma_{12} = 0$, then the conditional regression model (3.18) reduces to the form of the reserve-flow structural equation (3.14) and so estimation of (3.14) by ordinary least squares will yield the optimal estimators. This is so even though the government sterilizes reserve inflows and the reserve variable Granger-causes the domestic credit variable.

The general dynamic case

Some commentators have suggested that the true reserve-flow relationship may not be contemporaneous (e.g. Johannes, 1981; Argy, 1977). We therefore introduce a simple lag structure into the reserve-flow equation to see how the results are affected. If the reserve-flow equation is of the form:

$$r_t = ad_t + bd_{t-1} + cm_t + u_t \tag{3.19}$$

then a test of the MABP would presumably be:

$$H_o : a + b = 1.$$

Retaining the previous form of the dynamic reaction function:

$$d_t = \alpha d_{t-1} + \beta r_{t-1} + v_t \tag{3.20}$$

The reduced form consists of (3.20) and

$$r_t = (a\alpha + b)d_{t-1} + a\beta r_{t-1} + cm_t + \kappa_t$$

where:

$$\kappa_t = u_t + av_t$$

Hence:

$$\begin{bmatrix} \kappa_t \\ v_t \end{bmatrix} \sim IN \left[0, \begin{Bmatrix} \omega_{11} & \omega_{12} \\ \omega_{12} & \omega_{22} \end{Bmatrix} \right]$$

where:

$$\omega_{11} = \sigma_{11} + a^2\sigma_{22} + 2a\sigma_{12}$$
$$\omega_{22} = \sigma_{22}$$
$$\omega_{12} = a\sigma_{22} + \sigma_{12}$$

The conditional expectation of r_t then suggests the regression:

$$r_t = Ad_t + Bd_{t-1} + Cm_t + Dr_{t-1} + \pi_t \qquad (3.21)$$
$$\pi_t \sim N(o, \tau^2)$$

where

$$A = a + \sigma_{12}/\sigma_{22}$$
$$B = b - a\sigma_{12}/\sigma_{22}$$
$$C = c$$
$$D = -\beta\sigma_{12}/\sigma_{22}$$
$$\pi_t = r_t - E(r_t|d_t, r_{t-1})$$
$$\tau^2 = \sigma_{11} - \sigma_{12}^2/\sigma_{22}.$$

Again the crucial point from the point of view of ordinary least squares estimation is whether the structural disturbances are correlated, i.e. whether $\sigma_{12} = 0$. If so, then (3.21) reduces to the form (3.19) and estimation of (3.19) by ordinary least squares will yield consistent estimators even though the reserves variable Granger-causes the domestic credit variable and the reserve-flow equation is dynamic.

Conclusion on exogeneity

This section has examined the consequences for least squares estimation of the reserve-flow equation of the presence of systematic sterilization by the monetary authorities, and the possibility of detection of possible bias by Granger-type causality testing. It was found that only in the case of instantaneous sterilization of the reserve inflow (at least from the data perspective) did potential bias occur and in this case detection of reverse causation by Granger-type tests will be impossible, since there is, by definition, bidirectional feedback. Moreover, for a variety of assumptions about the dynamics of the data generating structure, it was found that the relevant estimators may be asymptotically unbiased when Granger causality runs from the reserve variable to the domestic credit variable, providing that the data generating structure is well specified in the sense that the stochastic disturbances are orthogonal.

A more fruitful way of testing the exogeneity specification might therefore be along the lines of test procedures for errors in variables first suggested by Liviatan (1963) and further developed by Wu (1973) and Hausman (1978) (see Taylor, 1987).

THE USE OF IDENTITIES IN THE EMPIRICAL MODEL OF THE MABP

In the MABP literature there seems to be a suspicion that the empirical model used for the reserve-flow equation might be dominated by a money stock identity. For example, Johnson argues:

> First, there is a dangerous temptation to test and confirm the monetary approach spuriously, by verifying statistically the tautology that an increase in domestic money must be provided either by domestic credit creation or by reserve acquisition (Johnson, 1977, p. 13).

Magee suggests that the estimated equation might be '. . . dominated by the central bank balance sheet identity . . . ' (Magee, 1976, p. 586).

A similar sentiment is also expressed by Frenkel *et al.* (1980), and by Kreinin and Officer (1978). In this part of the chapter we argue that this is indeed the case with most estimated reserve-flow equations. These studies in effect reproduce the original monetary base identity in disguise.

In section 1, where we derived the standard empirical model of the MABP, relation 3.3, the money supply process, was taken to be an identity:

$$M_s \equiv k(R + D) \qquad (3.3)$$

Given the level of reserves, domestic credit and the money supply ($M_s = M$), (3.3) essentially defines k:

$$k \equiv \frac{M}{(R+D)}$$

If k was given its own behavioural equation in terms of other exogenous variables, or else set equal to a constant, or even measured in some other way, then (3.3) would not be an exact and designed equality for all values of the variables concerned (i.e. an accounting identity) but a behavioural equation purporting to explain the money supply process.

In the exegetical literature k is often assumed to be constant (e.g. Magee, 1976; Johannes, 1981). This would imply, however, that $\Delta \ln k = 0$, so that it would drop out of the reserve-flow equation altogether. But in much of the applied literature $\Delta \ln k$ is included in the estimated equation (see Kreinin and Officer, 1978, ch. 7). The implication is that the estimated equation is made to revolve around the monetary base identity.

Differentiating (3.3) logarithmically and approximating the differential operator by the first difference operator:

$$\Delta \ln M = \Delta \ln k + \frac{\Delta R}{R+D} + \frac{\Delta D}{R+D}$$

Rearranging:

$$\frac{\Delta R}{R+D} = \Delta \ln M - \Delta \ln k - \frac{\Delta D}{R+D} \qquad (3.22)$$

Comparing (3.22) with (3.8), we can see that the latter has the term $(\eta_p \Delta \ln p + \eta_y \Delta \ln y + \eta_r \Delta \ln r)$ instead of $\Delta \ln M$. This implies that the estimated equation (3.9) is in fact nothing but the accounting identity (3.3) subject to the approximation error

$$e = \Delta \ln M - (\eta_p \Delta \ln p + \eta_y \Delta \ln y + \eta_r \Delta \ln r) \qquad (3.23)$$

and the smaller the approximation, the closer the estimated equation is to the identity. Hence, acceptance of the restrictions (3.10) should not in fact be interpreted as a confirmation of a set of theoretical propositions but as a test of how small the approximation error is. Moreover, the smallness of e does not depend on how good (3.5) is as a demand for money function — in the context of accounting identities the numbers dominate theoretical adequacy (see section 3.2). What matters is how good a proxy ($\eta_p \Delta \ln p$ + $\eta_y \Delta \ln y$ + $\eta_r \Delta \ln r$) is for the data $\Delta \ln M$. This differs from the diagnosis provided by Frenkel *et al.*, who suggest that although when (3.9) fits the data exactly, a_4 and a_5 are in effect estimates of minus unity: '. . . if the money demand equation were misspecified, all the estimates, including $\hat{b}_5$, could be biased . . . ' (1980, p. 586). It differs also from that of Kreinin and Officer who argue: '. . . the appropriate solution to these problems [the monetary base identity and sterilization] is to use a method like two-stage least-squares . . . ' (1978, p. 55).

Empirical Evidence Reconsidered

Let us consider the above arguments, using the following quarterly data for the UK 1965I–1971IV: R_t, international reserves; H_t, stock of high-powered money; M_t, money stock; $D_t \equiv (H_t - R_t)$, the domestic component of the monetary base; y_t, real GDP; p_t, implicit GDP deflator; r_t, gross redemption yield on UK government bonds issued at par with 20 years to maturity. (All data are quarterly and seasonally unadjusted and were obtained from the IMF International Financial Statistics data tape. Exact sources are listed in Appendix 5.1, except for r_t which is IFS line 61.)

Estimation of equation (3.9), using these data, yielded:

$$\frac{(\Delta \hat{R}_t)}{(R_t + D_t)} = \underset{(0.21)}{1.016} \, \Delta \ln p_t + \underset{(0.07)}{0.444} \, \Delta \ln y_t - \underset{(0.08)}{0.065} \, \Delta \ln r_t$$

$$- \underset{(0.13)}{1.08} \, \Delta \ln k_t - \underset{(0.08)}{0.994} \, \frac{(\Delta D_t)}{(R_t + D_t)} \qquad (3.24)$$

$$R^2 = 0.92, \ \bar{R}^2 = 0.90, \ s = 0.01645, \ DW = 2.00, \ T = 28.$$

Taking into consideration the fact that we use quarterly time series data and the estimated equation is relatively static (in growth terms) these results can only be described as very impressive both on statistical and theoretical grounds. All the coefficients have the sign and size expected *a priori* and all but a_3 are significantly different from zero. The DW statistic gives no indication of any systematic first-order dynamic effects in the residuals and all the restrictions in (3.10) are easily accepted. The argument above, however, suggests that (3.24) is in effect reproducing the accounting identity (3.3) subject to two approximation errors:

(i)   the error due to approximating the derivatives with first differences, and

(ii) the approximation error e_t.

In order to isolate these two sources of error (3.22) was estimated directly:

$$\frac{(\Delta \hat{R}_t)}{(R_t + D_t)} = \underset{(0.01)}{0.95} \Delta \ln M_t - \underset{(0.01)}{1.01} \Delta \ln k_t - \underset{(0.007)}{0.990} \frac{(\Delta D_t)}{(R_t + D_t)}$$

$$(3.25)$$

$$R^2 = 0.999, \ \bar{R}^2 = 0.999, \ s_1 = 0.0017, \ DW = 2.7, \ T = 28.$$

(3.25) is the accounting identity subject only to the first approximation error, which is rather small ($s_1{}^2 = 0.000003$). To isolate the second source of error the following equation was estimated:

$$\Delta \ln \tilde{M}_t = \underset{(0.2)}{1.06} \Delta \ln p_t + \underset{(0.07)}{0.453} \Delta \ln y_t - \underset{(0.08)}{0.070} \Delta \ln r_t$$

$$(3.26)$$

$$R^2 = 0.65, \ \bar{R}^2 = 0.60, \ s_2 = .01652, \ DW = 2.06, \ T = 28.$$

When the fitted values $\Delta \ln \tilde{M}_t$ were used in (3.22), estimation yielded:

$$\frac{(\Delta \hat{R}_t)}{(R_t + D_t)} = \underset{(0.12)}{0.932} \Delta \hat{\ln}M_t - \underset{(0.11)}{1.083} \Delta \ln k_t - \underset{(0.06)}{0.997} \frac{(\Delta D_t)}{(R_t + D_t)}$$

$$(3.27)$$

$$R^2 = 0.92, \bar{R}^2 = 0.91, s_3 = 0.01579, DW = 2.01, T = 28.$$

Comparing (3.27) with (3.24), we can see that the former virtually replicates the latter taking into account (3.26).

The question which naturally arises is to what extent the close reproduction of the accounting identity in (3.24) or (3.27) is an indication of how good (3.26) is as a demand for money. It might be argued, for example, that the MABP only works well with a well defined and stable demand function for money, and that only if this exists does the identity hold and the theory become a good predictor of reserve flows in response to domestic credit changes (see, for example, Genberg, 1976). As argued above, however, how well defined or stable the demand function for money is has no real bearing on how close to the identity (3.24) is. In order to see this consider the following rather 'Jevsonian' money demand equation:

$$\Delta \hat{\ln}M_t = \underset{(0.08)}{0.20} + \underset{(0.01)}{0.04} \Delta SS_t - \underset{(0.03)}{0.13} \Delta \ln SS_t$$
$$+ \underset{(0.01)}{0.02} \ln(SS/M)_{t-1} + \underset{(0.01)}{0.03} \Delta \ln RF_t \qquad (3.28)$$

$$R^2 = 0.63, \bar{R}^2 = 0.57, s = 0.01704, DW = 2.1, T = 28;$$

where SS_t and RF_t denote average daily sunshine and total rainfall (in England and Wales) respectively (source: *Annual Abstract of Statistics*). Clearly this cannot be interpreted as a well defined demand for money function, but when the fitted values of $\Delta \ln M_t$ are used in (3.22), it yields:

$$\frac{(\Delta \hat{R}_t)}{(R_t + D_t)} = \underset{(0.17)}{1.01} \Delta \hat{\ln}M_t - \underset{(0.11)}{1.13} \Delta \ln k_t - \underset{(0.07)}{1.07} \frac{(\Delta D_t)}{(R_t + D_t)}$$

$$(3.29)$$

$$R^2 = 0.92, \ \bar{R}^2 = 0.91, \ s_4 = 0.0155, \ DW = 2.2, \ T = 28.$$

If we compare (3.29) with (3.27), we can see that (3.28) performs better than (3.26) in terms of how closely the identity is recovered. Hence the theoretical validity of (3.26) is totally dominated by the smallness of the approximation error as measured by s_4 in (3.29). As for the contention that (3.24) can become a good predictor of ΔR_t, it ignores the fact that unless R_t is known, k_t is not available to be used in (3.24). But even if $\Delta \ln k_t$ were estimated, it would be preferable to substitute everything into (3.3) and calculate ΔR_t instead of estimating it.

In order to reinforce the argument that (3.24) is dominated by the accounting identity (3.3) let us consider dropping $\Delta \ln k_t$, as some expositions suggest. Re-estimation of (3.24) without $\Delta \ln k_t$ yielded:

$$\frac{(\Delta R_t)}{(R_t + D_t)} = \underset{(0.42)}{1.13} \Delta \ln p_t + \underset{(0.14)}{0.356} \Delta \ln y_t$$

$$- \underset{(0.16)}{0.293} \Delta \ln r_t - \underset{(0.09)}{0.49} \frac{(\Delta D_t)}{(R_t + D_t)} \qquad (3.30)$$

$$R^2 = 0.67, \ \bar{R}^2 = 0.62, \ s_5 = 0.0324, \ DW = 2.55, \ T = 28.$$

Apart from the dramatic fall in the goodness of fit and doubling of the standard error of the regression in comparison with (3.24), there are signs of dynamic misspecification and the estimated offset coefficient is significantly different from minus unity. As we pointed out in section 1, it is the nearness of this estimate to minus unity rather than its negativity which provides a test of the MABP against non-monetary alternatives.

CONCLUSION

The aim of this chapter was to take a critical look at some of the standard methods and results in the empirical literature on the monetary approach to the balance of payments.

In section 1 we derived a standard empirical model of the MABP. The following section then discussed potential sources of simultaneous equations bias in the standard reserve-flow equation. In particular we argued that the OLS estimate of the offset coefficient may be biased upwards in absolute value.

We then performed a Granger-type test of the exogeneity specification implicit in the standard empirical model of the MABP, using UK data. We were forced to reject the hypothesis of the joint exogeneity of the independent variables and in particular to question the exogeneity of the domestic credit variable. This accords with results reported by Johannes (1981), who also uses systems tests, and contrasts with those of Blejer (1979), who does not. However, following a discussion of the concept of exogeneity in the context of a regression model, we pointed out that the important criterion from the point of view of estimation was that of weak exogeneity, which is not at all the same thing as Granger non-causality (see, for example, Engle *et al.*, 1983). We then showed formally that under a variety of assumptions concerning the dynamic structure of the reserve-flow equation and a hypothesized government sterilization function, the presence or otherwise of Granger causality from the reserve variable to the domestic credit variable was irrelevant in the choice of estimator and that even when reserves did Granger-cause domestic credit, the ordinary least squares estimator may still retain its optimal properties. This does not mean, however, that Granger tests of causality are not useful. Our own results, together with those of Johannes, suggest that the monetary authorities in the UK and in several other European countries may in the past have attempted to sterilize lagged reserve inflows, and this by itself is empirically informative. Moreover, the presence of Granger causality from the dependent variables to the reserve flow variable implies that conditional forecasting using the OLS estimates is invalid. In fact, for efficient conditional forecasts we require weak exogeneity and Granger non-causality to hold simultaneously (Engle *et al.*, 1983).

In the second half of the chapter we discussed the use of identities in the empirical modelling process of the monetary approach, again illustrating the discussion by means of UK data.

We showed that the estimated standard reserve-flow equation in effect reproduces the money stock identity in disguise. In particular, this implies that the estimated offset coefficient, far from being an estimate of the reduced-form effect of the growth of domestic credit on the growth of reserves, is an estimate of minus unity. We also showed that the specification will tend to produce results supportive of the monetary approach irrespective of whether the implicit money demand function is correctly specified or stable or not. Treating the money multiplier as a constant and thereby avoiding the identities problem produced results which were not supportive of the MABP. Our conclusions from this section are clear-cut: much of the empirical literature of the MABP (for example, many of the studies cited by Magee, 1976, or included in Frenkel and Johnson, 1976) cannot be interpreted as providing unequivocal support for the monetary approach, as their authors suggest.

So far, our discussion of the empirical literature on the monetary approach does not escape the injunction of Frenkel and Johnson concerning purely negative criticism of the applied econometric work of others. A willingness to take up their challenge motivates a large part of the rest of the book. In the next chapter we consider a more general theoretical model of balance of payments determination which encompasses the monetary approach. We then derive an empirical model whilst attempting to avoid the potential pitfalls outlined above. Estimates of the model are reported in Chapter 5.

4. A Portfolio Balance Approach

INTRODUCTION

In Chapter 1 we gave an exposition and discussion of the monetary approach to balance of payments adjustment under fixed exchange rates (MABP). We discussed the relationship between the MABP and portfolio balance analyses of international capital movements and argued that, at least in most expositions, the monetary approach makes the implicit assumption that international capital is perfectly mobile. Up until now we have left the notion of perfect capital mobility deliberately vague. We have merely asserted that this assumption is tantamount to assuming that there is a single aggregate bond market which can be eliminated by Walras's Law. By assuming continuous market clearing on the real side, international monetarists are then able to concentrate their analysis solely on the money market.

The assumption of perfect capital mobility can in fact be broken down into two further assumptions. The first is that of instantaneous portfolio adjustment, i.e. that at each point in time actual portfolio holdings are equal to desired portfolio holdings. Since all of the data we shall use in our empirical analysis will be quarterly, this is probably not an unwarranted assumption — funds can be shifted about on the international capital markets in seconds with extremely low relative transactions costs. The second assumption is that of perfect substitutability between foreign and domestic bonds. Since we make the assumption of instantaneous portfolio adjustment, we shall treat the conditions of perfect capital mobility and perfect substitutability of foreign and domestic bonds as equivalent.

In this chapter we develop a general portfolio balance

model of balance of payments determination, which, whilst retaining the fundamental stock-flow distinction, relaxes the perfect substitution assumption of the MABP whilst retaining it as a special case. Our aim is to develop an empirical model which can then be confronted with the data.

A PORTFOLIO BALANCE APPROACH

The MABP as developed from Johnson (1958) is distinguished by its emphasis on stock equilibrium in the analysis of the international balancing process. This emphasis is shared by the approach to be outlined here, which we shall term the portfolio approach to the balance of payments (PABP). One area in which the two approaches do differ is in the implicit assumption in the MABP that domestic and foreign bonds are perfect substitutes in private portfolios; the PABP does away with this assumption and introduces bonds directly into the analysis. Our approach is thus a synthesis of the stock equilibrium approach to capital flows as developed from Branson (1968) and the MABP as outlined in Chapter 1.

Kouri and Porter (1974) attempt a similar synthesis in the context of a model of capital flows. The major difference between their model and the one developed here is that the former is primarily a model of capital flows, whereas ours is a model of overall balance of payments adjustment. In fact, a capital account equation is implicit in our analysis and is netted out to obtain an overall balance of payments equation.

The model developed is an extremely simple one and accordingly has to make a number of simplifying assumptions. In particular, since we are concerned with the mechanism through which equilibrium is attained in the financial markets of a small open economy, it is assumed that most markets on the real side clear continuously at levels ground out at Walrasian equilibrium (perhaps with friction); we also assume that there is no feedback from the financial side onto these equilibrium levels. To some extent this can be viewed as an abstraction from certain features of the real world in order to obtain as simple and as analytically tractable a model as possible; a first criterion of both economic and econometric modelling should be 'to strip models of unnecessary and frivolous generality' (Dornbusch, 1980, p. 6). Since the period we wish to analyse is the decade leading up to the breakdown of the adjustable peg system in the early 1970s, this may be seen as a useful working assumption.

Moreover, we are essentially concerned with taking up the challenge cast down by Frenkel and Johnson which we alluded to in the introductory chapter. That is, given as our starting point a general Chicago *Weltanschauung*, we want to illustrate how, in our view, one should go about the modelling and estimation processes. Further, since the model we are developing is explicitly in the Chicago tradition, an appeal might be made to Chicago methodology (see, for example, Friedman, 1953), neatly summed up by Begg: 'Economic theory necessarily involves some simplification. Useful theories make powerful simplications to yield sharp predictions which are not falsified by the data' (1982, p. 69).

Consider a small open economy with three fiat assets which are gross substitutes in domestic portfolios: domestic bonds A, foreign bonds B*, and money M. Foreign bonds are internationally traded and are assumed to be in perfectly elastic supply at the foreign rate of interest. Domestic bonds can be thought of as arising from past deficits in the government budget and may not be traded internationally (hence avoiding the possibility that the authorities will finance a trade deficit by open market operations). We assume bonds to be of a fixed-price-variable-coupon type and that the private sector does not discount or capitalize future taxes or transfers (hence changes in interest rates do not affect bond prices). Further, we avoid the problems raised in the last chapter by taking the money multiplier to be a constant (unity in fact, although this is of no qualitative importance) or equivalently that money demand is a demand for a high-powered stock. None of these simplifying assumptions qualitatively affect our results but do significantly simplify the algebra.

The starting point for our analysis is the specification of short-run asset demand functions along lines originally suggested by Tobin (1969) (see Dornbusch, 1975; Ujiie, 1978).

The portfolio behaviour relations we posit are as follows.

Money demand:

$$M = \ell(r, r^*, y)W; \tag{4.1}$$
$$\ell_r < 0, \ell_{r^*} < 0, \ell_y > 0;$$
$$\eta_r < 0, \eta_{r^*} < 0, \eta_y > 0.$$

Demand for domestic bonds:

$$B = b(r, r^*, y)W; \tag{4.2}$$
$$b_r > 0, b_{r^*} < 0, b_y < 0;$$
$$\lambda_r > 0, \lambda_{r^*} < 0, \lambda_y < 0.$$

Demand for foreign bonds:

$$B^* = b^*(r, r^*, y)W; \tag{4.3}$$
$$b^*_r < 0, b^*_{r^*} > 0, b^*_y < 0;$$
$$\mu_r < 0, \mu_{r^*} > 0, \mu_y < 0.$$

where: $r = (1 + i)/(1 + \dot{p})$;
 i = domestic nominal interest rate;
 $\dot{p}$ = rate of change of domestic prices;
 $r^* = (1 + i^*)/(1 + \dot{p})$;
 i^* = foreign nominal interest rate;
 y = domestic real income;
 W = private sector net wealth,
  $= [M + B + B^*]$

The b_i's, b^*_i's and ℓ_i's denote first derivatives, whilst the η_i's, λ_i's and μ_i's denote elasticities.

The arguments and partial derivatives of the demand functions need little comment (see, for example, Tobin, 1969). Note, however, that real income enters all three functions through the transactions demand for money and consequent portfolio reallocation. The functions are homogeneous in prices (through homogeneity in nominal wealth) and real wealth. The homogeneity assumptions, due to Tobin (1969), allow us to put some structure on this very general formulation by yielding certain adding up restrictions which we shall discuss presently.

It might be argued that the functions should include a variable to capture exchange rate expectations, as, for example, in Gylfason and Helliwell, 1983. However, given the discontinuities of exchange rate changes within an adjustable peg regime, it is not clear how such expectations should be either modelled or measured. We therefore chose to assume static expectations in our theoretical model and use dummy variables to handle the problem in our empirical analysis.

On the supply side of the model we have the money supply relation (now a behavioural equation):

$$M = R + D; \tag{4.4}$$

$$\sigma_R = R/M > 0, \sigma_D = D/M > 0$$

where σ_R and σ_D denote trivial supply elasticities with respect to reserves and domestic credit. Foreign bonds are assumed not to be held as reserves.

The level of domestic bonds is given by:

$$A = B + D \tag{4.5}$$

where B represents domestic bonds held by the private sector and D represents the level of domestic bonds held by the monetary authorities (which is equal to the level of domestic credit).

If we assume a balanced government budget and denote time derivatives by dots:

$$\dot{A} = 0 = \dot{B} + \dot{D} \tag{4.6}$$

$$\Rightarrow \dot{B} = -\dot{D}$$

$$\Rightarrow \hat{B} = -a\hat{D} \tag{4.7}$$

where a circumflex denotes a growth rate and $a = D/B$.

The homogeneity properties of the asset demand functions can now be utilized to yield the following adding up restrictions.

Adding up:

$$\ell + b + b^* = 1;$$
$$\ell_j + b_j + b^*_j = 0, (j = r, r^*, y);$$
$$\ell\eta_j + b\lambda_j + b^*\mu_j = 0, (j = r, r^*, y).$$

Differentiating the asset demand functions logarithmically with respect to time, using the adding up conditions and making use of a domestic bond market equilibrium condition to eliminate the domestic interest rate, we derive:

$$R = -\frac{(a\eta_r + \sigma_D\lambda_r)}{(\lambda_r\sigma_R)}\hat{D} + \frac{(\lambda_r\eta_y - \lambda_y\eta_r)}{(\lambda_r\sigma_R)}\hat{y}$$

$$+ \frac{(\lambda_r - \eta_r)}{(\lambda_r\sigma_R)}\hat{W} + \frac{(\lambda_r\eta_{r^*} - \lambda_{r^*}\eta_r)}{(\lambda_r\sigma_R)}\hat{r}^*$$

or

$$\hat{R} = \beta_1\hat{D} + \beta_2\hat{y} + \beta_3\hat{W} + \beta_4\hat{r}^* \tag{4.8}$$

Using the signs of elasticities, we can deduce the signs of the coefficients of $\hat{r}^*$ and $\hat{W}$:

$$\beta_3 > 0, \beta_4 < 0$$

Using the adding up restriction

$$\ell\eta_r + b\lambda_r + b^*\mu_r = 0,$$

the coefficient of $\hat{D}$ may be rewritten:

$$\beta_1 = \frac{\sigma_D}{\sigma_R}\frac{B^*\mu_r}{B\lambda_r} \tag{4.9}$$

Empirically, it seems reasonable to make the approximation $\sigma_D/\sigma_R \approx 1$, so that, since as we approach perfect capital mobility:

$$\mu_r \; \rightarrow \; -\infty$$

and:

$$\lambda_r \; \rightarrow \; +\infty$$

then we have:

$$\beta_1 \; \rightarrow \; -1$$

This suggests, firstly, that β_1 lies in the closed interval $[-1, 0]$ and, secondly, that this coefficient will approach minus unity as the level of capital mobility increases. Intuitively, a value of β_1 of minus unity simply means that the demand for domestic bonds will not be well defined: agents will have an overall target level of the stock of bonds they wish to hold but will be indifferent to the composition of that stock between foreign and domestic bonds. Thus, changes in the growth of domestic bonds will be offset one-to-one by changes in the growth of foreign bond holding and domestic monetary policy will reduce to 'pushing on a string'. In this case (4.8) will in fact be a form of the MABP reserve-flow equation. On the other hand, when foreign and domestic bonds are perfectly non-substitutable, $\mu_r = 0$ and so $\beta_1 = 0$ — reserve flows will only be affected by changes in the level of domestic credit through portfolio extent effects, i.e. through W. Intermediate levels of substitutability suggest a value of the offset coefficient between zero and minus unity.

By a similar argument we can rewrite the coefficient of y:

$$\beta_2 \; = \; \frac{B^*}{R} \; \frac{(\lambda_y \mu_r - \lambda_r \mu_y)}{\lambda_r} > 0 \tag{4.10}$$

Thus we can write:

$$\hat{R} \; = \; \beta_1 \hat{D} + \beta_2 \hat{y} + \beta_3 \hat{W} + \beta_4 \hat{r}^* \tag{4.11}$$

with

$$-1 < \beta_1 < 0, \beta_2 > 0, \beta_3 > 0, \beta_4 < 0.$$

Thus far, however, our equation is empirically non-operational because of the difficulty in measuring $\dot{W}$ (Kouri and Porter simply drop all wealth variables from their estimated equation). However, differentiating the portfolio behaviour functions with respect to time and using adding up, we can obtain:

$$OBP = \dot{R} = (b^*_r/b_r)\dot{D} + W(\ell_y - b_y\ell_r/b_r)\dot{y}$$
$$+ (\ell - b\ell_r/b_r)\dot{W} + W(\ell_{r*} - b_{r*}\ell_r/b_r)\dot{r}^* \quad (4.12)$$

which, as an expression for the rate of change of reserves, is an overall balance of payments equation (OBP). Similarly, by noting that the rate of change of domestic holdings of foreign assets is the obverse of the capital account, we can derive a capital account equation:

$$CAP = -\dot{B}^* = (b^*_r/b_r)\dot{D} + W(b_y b^*_r/b_r - b^*_y)\dot{y}$$
$$+ (bb^*_r/b_r - b^*)\dot{W} + W(b_{r*} b^*_r/b_r - b^*_{r*})\dot{r}^*$$
$$(4.13)$$

Now, using adding up it is easily seen that the CAP and OBP equations have identical coefficients except for the coefficients of $\dot{W}$, which differ by unity:

$$(\ell - b\ell_r/b_r) - (bb^*_r/b_r - b^*)$$
$$= (b_r\ell - b\ell_r - bb^*_r + b^*b_r)/b_r$$
$$= (b_r\ell + b(b_r + b^*_r) - bb^*_r + b^*b_r)/b_r$$
$$= \ell + b + b^*$$
$$= 1$$

And since the current account balance (CAB) is nothing but the difference between the overall balance of payments and the capital account:

$$CAB = OBP - CAP = \dot{W} \quad (4.14)$$

Thus, in this model changes in wealth are related one-to-one with the current account. This follows directly from our assumption of a static level of domestic bonds and abstraction from consideration of physical capital.

We assume a stable relationship between nominal income (Y) and net wealth:

$$Y = \gamma W \qquad (4.15)$$

Hence:

$$\hat{W} = \gamma(CAB/Y). \qquad (4.16)$$

Then we can write:

$$\hat{R} = \beta_1 \hat{D} + \beta_2 \hat{y} + \beta_3 (CAB/Y) + \beta_4 \hat{r}^* \qquad (4.17)$$

where β_3 is appropriately redefined. At first sight it may appear strange to include a current account balance term in an equation purporting to explain the overall balance of payments. Recall, however, our assumption of exogeneity of the real or flow side of the economy. Given that output is at or near its natural level or steady-state growth path, the current account will be determined primarily by the level of domestic absorption. The underlying assumption is that agents will alter the level of absorption in order to achieve the long-run target level of the stock of wealth. Under these assumptions CAB/Y will be exogenous for $\hat{R}$.

Further,

$$\hat{r}^* = \frac{\partial \ln r^*}{\partial t} = \frac{\partial}{\partial t} (\ln(1 + i^*) - \ln(1 + \dot{p})).$$

For small i^* and p:

$$\hat{r}^* = \frac{\partial}{\partial t} (i^* - \dot{p})$$

$$= \dot{d}, \text{ say.}$$

Hence:

$$\hat{R} = \beta_1 \hat{D} + \beta_2 \hat{y} + \beta_3 (CAB/Y) + \beta_4 \dot{d}$$
$$-1 < \beta_1 < 0, \beta_2 > 0, \beta_3 > 0, \beta_4 < 0 \qquad (4.18)$$

CONCLUSION

In this chapter we have derived a putative reduced form balance of payments equation (4.18), which includes as arguments the growth in the domestic component of the monetary base, the rate of growth of real income, the current account balance in proportion to the level of domestic income and the change in the foreign interest rate adjusted for domestic inflation. The first two and the last terms capture portfolio allocation effects whilst the third term introduces portfolio extent effects. The theoretical underpinning of the equation is similar to the monetary approach to the balance of payments except that no assumptions are made concerning the degree of international capital mobility. As international capital mobility approaches perfection, the coefficient of the domestic credit variable approaches minus unity and (4.18) collapses to a form of the MABP reserve-flow equation.

By an argument precisely analogous to the one discussed in Chapter 3, it can be shown that if sterilization is present through a reaction function which relates the growth in the domestic credit component of the monetary base linearly to the growth in reserves and other variables, then the OLS estimate of β_1 will be biased towards minus unity. Care must therefore be exercised in interpreting the offset coefficient.

Apart from the question as to whether or not (4.18) constitutes a reduced form equation, concern may be expressed at the method of linearization in its derivation. In particular, the implication is that the β's may be treated as constants for the purposes of estimation whereas in fact they are functions of certain elasticities and partial derivatives which themselves would be endogenous in a more completely specified model. Moreover, the offset coefficient on the domestic credit variable may be interpreted as an indicator of the degree of international capital mobility by its distance from minus unity and this could therefore hardly be expected to remain constant over a period such as the 1960s or 1970s. Thus, one might expect at least a subset of the coefficients to vary systematically or otherwise over time. In answer to this we could point to examples in the literature where equations have been derived in a similar fashion and the coefficients treated as constant for the purposes of estimation (see, for example, Kouri and Porter, 1974). This seems an over-strong assumption, however, and in the next chapter we present estimation results obtained by allowing the parameters to vary over time in a number of ways.

5. Multi-Country Econometric Evidence on the Portfolio Balance Approach

INTRODUCTION

In the last chapter we derived a general portfolio balance model of balance of payments determination which nests the monetary approach as a special case (perfect capital mobility). The purpose of the present chapter is to present the results of statistical and econometric analysis of this model, using data for several major OECD countries.

The empirical model developed in Chapter 4 was as follows:

$$\hat{R} = \beta_0 + \beta_1 \hat{D} + \beta_2 \hat{y} + \beta_3 \, \text{CAB}/Y + \beta_4 \dot{d} \qquad (5.1)$$

where our priors are:

$$\beta_0 = 0; -1 < \beta_1 < 0; \beta_2 > 0; \beta_3 > 0; \beta_4 < 0; \qquad (5.2)$$

and where:

$\hat{R}$ = growth rate of reserves;
$\hat{D}$ = growth rate of domestic credit;
$\hat{y}$ = growth rate of domestic real income;
Y = domestic nominal income;
CAB = current account balance;
$\dot{d}$ = $(i^* - \dot{p})$;
i^* = foreign interest rate;
$\dot{p}$ = domestic rate of inflation.

Recall that the linearization of the theoretical model in

order to obtain the form (5.1) implied that the coefficients may be time-varying, although, with the possible exception of β_1, there appeared to be no clear theoretical basis for determining a systematic model of parameter variation.

The offset coefficient β_1 was, however, expected to vary according to the degree of international capital mobility and lie in the closed interval between zero (implying zero capital mobility) and minus unity (implying perfect capital mobility). Thus, if the model were estimated over a period which witnessed a substantial shift in the degree of capital mobility, this parameter should vary over the sample period. This facet of our model is tested, using 1960s and early 1970s data and varying parameter estimation techniques based on the Kalman filter.

In the next section we discuss the historical background to the estimation period, before going on to present our empirical results in the following sections.

HISTORICAL BACKGROUND

The period following the establishment of the International Monetary Fund up until the breakdown of the adjustable peg system in the early 1970s was one of intense change in international political and economic relations. In the political arena there was a shift in the centre of mass of the Western power base towards the United States and a chilling of East–West relations. The steady, increasing US involvement in Vietnam during the 1960s, together with an increasing demand for international liquidity, contributed to the tendency towards persistent US deficits on the external account and a consequent increase in overseas holdings of dollars. The 1960s in particular were marked by a number of domestic political tensions and changes in the Western nations, characterized by the French student–worker riots or 'événements de mai' of 1968. Many of these political developments had counterparts or repercussions in the economic sphere. Thus, the period witnessed the gradual establishment of the US dollar as the reserve currency, as the gap left in reserve creation at the Bretton Woods Conference was filled by the flow of dollars into Europe as part of the Marshall Aid Program and chronic US deficits. Large overseas dollar holdings, together with controls on US capital markets through such measures as Regulation Q, led to the rise of the Eurodollar market from the late 1950s. The establishment of the Eurodollar market and later the Eurocurrency markets contributed greatly to the increase in capital mobility over the period; indeed a major attraction of the offshore capital markets was their immunity from exchange controls and other regulation.

Over the period 1950–71 the value of world trade increased more than five-fold (Williamson, 1977), bringing with it enlarged scope for shifting funds via the leading and lagging of payments. Similarly, the period saw a marked rise in the dominance of multinational corporations (Whitman, 1974, for example, reports that the earning on US foreign direct investment increased from $1.8 billion in 1950 to $10.3 billion in 1971) and hence of increased opportunities for transfer pricing. One might also refer in general terms to the increasing integration of financial markets and scope for arbitrage, facilitated by improvements in the communications network and information dissemination through international news and financial services agencies and other media.

This rise in capital mobility, coupled with the various political tensions of the late 1960s, led to various exchange rate crises — notably the dollar–gold crisis of 1968, the Canadian dollar crisis of 1968, the franc–mark crisis of 1968-9, and the continuing sterling crises from 1964 until the 1967 devaluation (see, for example, Krause, 1970). Williamson notes that 'By the time that the adjustable peg was abandoned, capital mobility had developed to the point where the Bundesbank could take in well over $1 billion in an hour when the market had come to expect that another parity change was impending' (Williamson, 1977, p. 50).

The international financial scene of the late 1960s was marked by a degree of capital mobility which had not been foreseen at the Bretton Woods Conference, and with which the international monetary system had not been designed to cope.

DATA

In order to make (5.1) estimateable with discrete (quarterly) observations, the differential operator can be approximated by the first difference operator and instantaneous growth rates by first differences in natural logarithms. In each case the 'foreign' interest rate was proxied by the US Treasury Bill Rate. A detailed listing of data sources can be found in Appendix 5.1.

Since the theoretical model from which (5.1) was derived makes the assumption of a fixed exchange rate regime, a data set extending beyond 1971 is really inappropriate. Estimation was therefore carried out, using data for the period 1964II–1971IV, for the UK, Germany, Italy, Canada, Japan and Australia (although this period overlaps slightly with the float of the Canadian dollar, experiments revealed little difference in our results and did not in our view warrant further truncation of the data set; this problem was in fact handled by means of dummy variables).

It is well known that the period of the 1960s and early 1970s was marked by a number of exchange rate crises caused by intense speculation concerning shifts in the official parities (see, for example, Krause, 1970). As we pointed out in Chapter 4, the theoretical underpinning of our empirical model takes no account of exchange rate expectations. Owing to the discontinuous nature of exchange rate changes under an adjustable peg regime, an appropriate approach to the problem might be by the use of dummy variables during periods of known heavy speculation in the foreign exchange and international capital markets. However, some of the estimators we use are highly non-linear and it is therefore desirable to limit the dimensions of the parameter space in order to facilitate discovery of the likelihood maxima. The method we chose therefore was to adjust each of the variables by regressing them individually on the appropriate dummies and using the residual vector as the adjusted variable. Intuitively, the adjusted variables will be purged of any elements peculiar to the period in question. Formally, it is easy to show that, at least for the linear estimators we use, this procedure is identically equivalent to including the dummy variables in a regression using the unadjusted variables (the Frisch–Waugh theorem — see, for example, Maddala, 1977, p. 462). The dummies for each country concerned are defined in Appendix 5.2, where we also reference the sources used in the identification of speculative periods.

CONSTANT PARAMETERS AND STERILIZATION

Estimation of (5.1) by an OLS projection using UK data yielded:

$$\hat{R} = 2.99 - 0.62\hat{D} + 0.66\hat{y} + 0.64\text{CAB}/Y - 3.38\dot{d} \qquad (5.3)$$
$$(2.41)(0.12) \quad (0.43) \quad (1.89) \qquad (3.18)$$

$$R^2 = 0.58; \bar{R}^2 = 0.51; DW = 1.95; D4 = 1.79; ES(4) = 3.27$$

$$SER = 9.28; T = 31.$$

Estimation using West German data yielded:

$$\hat{R} = 2.06 - 0.13\hat{D} + 2.21\hat{y} + 2.36\text{CAB}/Y - 3.04\dot{d} \qquad (5.4)$$
$$(1.87)(0.02) \quad (1.05) \quad (4.16) \qquad (2.54)$$

$$R^2 = 0.68; \bar{R}^2 = 0.63; DW = 1.83; D4 = 1.75; ES(4) = 3.02$$

$$SER = 7.60; T = 31.$$

D4 is Wallis's test statistic for fourth-order serial correlation (Wallis, 1972); ES(4) is an efficient score test statistic for fourth-order serial correlation, asymptotically distributed under the null of no autocorrelation as a central chi-square with four degrees of freedom. The values of DW, D4 and ES(4) for both equations tend to indicate that (5.1) is not dynamically misspecified and that it may in fact be a long-run reduced form.

All of the priors (5.2) are satisfied statistically for both sets of data, although the coefficients on the current account term and the interest rate variable are not in fact significantly different from zero. For each of the estimated equations, the 95 per cent confidence interval for the offset coefficient on the domestic credit variable is a proper subset of the prior unit interval [-1, 0] but excludes the lower bound of minus unity — thus apparently rejecting the monetary hypothesis of perfect capital mobility. The German estimated offset co-efficient is less than a quarter of the corresponding point estimate for the UK, perhaps reflecting institutional differences between the London and Frankfurt capital markets during this period. Overall, the German equation performs better than the UK estimation in terms of goodness of fit and the significance of coefficients.

In the presence of sterilization, the estimate of the offset coefficient may be biased upwards in absolute value (see Chapter 3). This suggests that an appropriate method of estimation may be by instrumental variables (IV), but this of course introduces the problem of choosing an appropriate set of instruments. However, if we assume that sterilization takes place within the quarter (since this is the only way that bias will be introduced into the OLS estimates), then lagged values of the domestic credit variable are appropriate instruments. In fact, we included the level and growth of domestic credit lagged up to three periods in the instrument set as well as the other regressors as instruments for themselves.

IV estimation of (5.1) for UK data yielded:

$$\hat{R} = 5.15 - 0.31\hat{D} + 0.44\hat{y} + 2.40\text{CAB/Y} - 3.56\dot{d} \qquad (5.5)$$
$$(2.82)(0.14) \quad (0.48) \quad (2.22) \qquad (3.51)$$
$$\text{SER} = 10.37; \text{DW} = 1.73; \text{IV}(5) = 6.09; \text{T} = 31$$

and for German data:

$$\hat{R} = 2.05 - 0.13\hat{D} + 2.21\hat{y} + 2.36\text{CAB/Y} - 3.05\dot{d} \qquad (5.6)$$
$$(1.96)(0.04) \quad (1.07) \quad (4.20) \qquad (2.64)$$
$$\text{SER} = 7.60; \text{DW} = 1.82; \text{IV}(5) = 10.00; \text{T} = 31.$$

The statistic IV(5) is from a test for the legitimacy of the instruments, due to Sargan (1958):

$$\text{IV}(m-k) = \frac{e'Z(Z'Z)^{-1}Z'e}{s^2} \qquad (5.7)$$

where Z is the (Txm) instrument set, k the number of regressors, e the estimated residual vector from the OLS regression and s^2 a consistent estimator of the true error variance. Under the null that Z is correlated with the set of regressors but orthogonal to the error:

$$IV(m-k) \underset{a}{\sim} X^2(m-k)$$

From (5.7) it is clear that IV(m-k) can be computed as

$$IV(m-k) = (T-m)R_a^2$$

where R_a^2 is the coefficient of determination from an auxiliary regression of the estimated residuals from the original regression on the instrument set. The critical level of the chi-square distribution with five degrees of freedom at a nominal size of 5 per cent is 11.1; in both cases the instrument sets are not rejected.

The effects of IV estimation for the two sets of data are quite different. For the German data there is virtually no discernible effect of allowing for the possible endogeneity of the domestic credit variable. For the UK, on the other hand, there is a dramatic drop in the absolute value of the estimate of the offset coefficient. More generally, the sizes of the estimated coefficients in (5.5) are more in line with those of the German equation. Intuitively therefore the empirical evidence appears to support the hypothesis that sterilization bias was a problem for the UK data over the period in question but is not apparent from the German data.

A formal test for the presence of within-the-period sterilization, based on the differences between the IV and OLS estimates and due to Hausman (1978), may be carried out as follows. Consider the regression model

$$Y = X_1 a_1 + X_2 a_2 + \epsilon$$

where the X_1 variables are possibly correlated with the disturbance, whilst the X_2 variables are known to be orthogonal to ϵ. Given a matrix of instruments Z (including X_2) which are correlated with X_1 but orthogonal to ϵ, we can compute

$$\hat{X}_1 = Z(Z'Z)^{-1}Z'X_1$$

— the orthogonal projection of X_1 onto the instrument set. Hausman then shows that in the regression:

$$Y = X_1 a_1 + X_2 a_2 + \hat{X}_1 a_3 + v$$

a test of $H_0 : a_3 = 0$ is equivalent to testing whether X_1 is orthogonal to ϵ (see Hausman, 1978, pp. 1259–60).

Adding the predicted values of the domestic credit variable from a regression on the instrument set into the original equation we obtained for the UK:

$$\hat{R} = 5.15 - 1.04\hat{D} + 0.44\hat{y} + 2.40CAB/Y - 3.56\dot{d} + 0.73\widetilde{D}$$
$$\phantom{\hat{R} = }(2.10)(0.16)\quad(0.36)\quad(1.66)\qquad(2.65)\quad(0.21)$$

$$(5.8)$$

and for Germany:

$$\hat{R} = 2.05 - 0.13\hat{D} + 2.21\hat{y} + 2.35CAB/Y - 3.05\dot{d} + 0.0004\widetilde{D}$$
$$\phantom{\hat{R} = }(2.00)(0.02)\quad(1.09)\quad(4.29)\qquad(2.69)\quad(0.0453)$$

$$(5.9)$$

where $\widetilde{D}$ is the fitted value. Clearly, the hypothesis of no contemporaneous correlation of $\widetilde{D}$ with the error term cannot be rejected for the German data at any reasonable level of significance, but is easily rejected for the UK.

This result for the UK is perhaps not surprising in view of our discussion of possible automatic sterilization through the Exchange Equalization Account in Chapter 3. The result for Germany is, however, in direct conflict with evidence presented by Obstfeld (1982) for a similar period. He analyses a capital-flow equation due to Kouri and Porter (1974) which is in many ways similar to the specification (5.1) except that the dependent variable is capital flow and growth rates are replaced with first differences. Just as the large difference in the OLS and IV estimates of the offset coefficients in our equations suggest that sterilization may have been present for the UK, Obstfeld argues that the differences in his estimates support the hypothesis of sterilization bias for Germany over a similar period. However, the differences in Obstfeld's co-efficient estimates are more likely due to the inappropriate-ness of his instruments (lagged inflation and the lagged percentage change in manufacturing orders) than to the presence of sterilization. An IV estimator is approximately consistent only if the covariance of the instruments with the error is small relative to the covariance with the observed explanatory variables. How small 'small' is may be determined approximately in finite samples using IV(m-k). Obstfeld supplies only perfunctory arguments for the choice of his instruments. Obstfeld (ibid.) also applies the Hausman test to conclude that the German authorities successfully pursued instantaneous sterilization policies throughout the 1960s. It is almost superfluous to point out that this test is conditional upon the maintained hypothesis that Z is an appropriate set of instruments.

All of the above regressions were also estimated using data for Italy, Canada, Japan, and Australia. Results are reported in Table 5.1.

As far as the simple OLS results are concerned, the equation performs tolerably well for all countries except Italy. The priors (5.2) are satisfied statistically, although some coefficients are occasionally insignificantly different from zero.

For Japan and Australia OLS estimation yielded a strongly significant but quite small offset coefficient –

-0.34 and -0.38
(0.07)   (0.06)

respectively. These results again suggest that the pure monetary approach is invalid. Again with the exception of Italy, IV estimation, and more formally the Hausman test, imply that the hypothesis of no contemporaneous sterili-zation of reserve inflows can be accepted at quite high levels of significance, certainly greater than 5 per cent.

Estimation with Canadian data yielded a significant and high point estimate of the offset coefficient – -0.81. The IV
(0.32)

and Hausman regressions again suggest the absence of con-temporaneous sterilization. The high value of the offset

Table 5.1 Constant parameter results for the single-equation model

Country	Method	$\hat{D}$	$\hat{y}$	CAB/y	$\dot{d}$	$\bar{D}$	R^2	$\bar{R}^2$	SER	DW	D4	ES(4)	IV(5)
UK	OLS	-0.62 (0.12)	0.66 (0.43)	0.64 (1.89)	-3.38 (3.18)	–	0.58	0.51	9.28	1.95	1.79	3.27	–
	IV	-0.31 (0.14)	0.44 (0.48)	2.40 (2.22)	-3.56 (3.51)	–	–	–	10.37	1.73	–	–	6.09
	Hausman	-1.04 (0.16)	0.44 (0.36)	2.40 (1.66)	-3.56 (2.65)	0.73 (0.21)	0.71	0.66	7.73	1.88	–	–	–
Germany	OLS	-0.13 (0.02)	2.21 (1.05)	2.36 (4.16)	-3.04 (2.54)	–	0.68	0.63	7.60	1.83	1.75	3.02	–
	IV	-0.13 (0.04)	2.21 (1.07)	2.36 (4.20)	-3.05 (2.64)	–	–	–	7.60	1.82	–	–	10.00
	Hausman	-0.13 (0.02)	2.21 (1.09)	2.35 (4.29)	-3.05 (2.69)	0.0004 (0.045)	0.68	0.62	7.75	1.82	–	–	–
Italy	OLS	-0.05 (0.08)	-0.13 (0.81)	5.74 (3.08)	-3.56 (2.22)	–	0.17	0.04	5.98	1.76	1.84	2.85	–
	IV	0.07 (0.10)	0.04 (0.85)	6.63 (3.25)	-3.88 (2.33)	–	–	–	6.25	1.65	–	–	4.65
	Hausman	-0.31 (0.13)	0.04 (0.74)	6.63 (2.84)	-3.88 (2.04)	0.38 (0.15)	0.33	0.20	5.46	1.93	–	–	–
Canada	OLS	-0.81 (0.32)	0.15 (0.06)	4.24 (3.12)	-0.46 (0.25)	–	0.69	0.64	6.23	2.24	1.64	8.20	–
	IV	-0.78 (0.34)	0.14 (0.08)	5.42 (3.48)	-1.14 (1.06)	–	–	–	6.65	2.23	–	–	3.13
	Hausman	-0.78 (0.35)	0.14 (0.08)	5.42 (3.22)	-1.14 (1.16)	0.11 (0.08)	0.72	0.68	6.15	2.61	–	–	–

Japan	OLS	-0.34 (0.07)	0.32 (1.30)	3.89 (0.71)	-2.62 (3.56)	—	0.63	0.57	9.86	1.46	1.25	6.41	—
	IV	-0.30 (0.08)	0.49 (1.31)	3.75 (0.73)	-1.90 (3.62)	—	—	—	9.94	1.44	—	—	7.79
	Hausman	-0.61 (0.18)	0.49 (1.26)	3.75 (0.70)	-1.90 (3.48)	0.33 (0.20)	0.67	0.60	9.55	1.38	—	—	—
Australia	OLS	-0.38 (0.06)	0.50 (0.76)	7.60 (3.28)	-1.17 (1.73)	—	0.72	0.68	5.17	2.17	1.26	5.29	—
	IV	-0.38 (0.09)	0.50 (0.76)	7.65 (3.47)	-1.18 (1.74)	—	—	—	5.17	2.17	—	—	7.67
	Hausman	-0.38 (0.07)	0.50 (0.78)	7.65 (3.54)	-1.18 (1.78)	0.005 (0.120)	0.72	0.67	5.28	2.17	—	—	—

coefficient — which is insignificantly different from minus unity — reflects the high degree of capital market integration between the United States and Canada (recall that the 'foreign' interest rate was proxied by the 3-month US Treasury Bill Rate).

The poor performance of the Italian equation is probably due to the perennial problem of the poorness of Italian data rather than anything else. Therefore, although the IV and Hausman results tend to indicate that sterilization was present, they are really inconclusive. It should be noted, however, that even with the Italian estimates, the priors (5.2) are strongly satisfied statistically.

TESTING FOR STRUCTURAL STABILITY

The cusum and cusumsq tests due to Brown, Durbin and Evans (1975) (BDE), which are designed to detect parameter variation, were computed for each of the countries concerned. Table 5.2 lists the maximum absolute value of the cusum for each country and the maximum deviation of the cumulative sum of squares from its mean value.

Table 5.2 Tests for structural stability

	Cusum	Cusumsq
UK	0.37	0.27
Germany	0.52	0.50*
Italy	0.70	0.37*
Canada	0.53	0.30
Japan	0.76	0.44*
Australia	0.57	0.39*

*Significant at 5 per cent level.

As can be seen from the table, the cusum test does not lead to rejection of the hypothesis of parameter stability for any of the countries at any reasonable level of significance (the critical value at the 10 per cent level being 0.85). On the other hand, the cusumsq test rejects the null for all countries except the UK and Canada at the 5 per cent level (the critical value being 0.32). In the light of Garbade's (1977) Monte Carlo evidence, this may well be symptomatic of the low power of the cusum test; on the other hand, it may indicate a shift in residual variance rather than in the regression coefficients (BDE, p. 159).

Plots of the cusum and cusumsq are given for the UK and Germany in Figures 5.1 to 5.4. BDE argue that the cusum and cusumsq techniques should be used in the spirit of data analysis. Thus, as they point out (pp. 154–5), the constructed significance lines should be regarded as 'yardsticks' against which to assess the observed trajectory rather than as formal tests of significance.

As far as the UK data are concerned, neither the cusum nor the cusumsq plots show any real marked tendency to move away from their respective mean value lines (neither in fact crosses a 10 per cent significance line). The plots for the German data are far more interesting. Whilst the cusum plot at no time crosses even a 10 per cent significance line, there appears to be a very marked move away from the mean value line around the nineteenth or twentieth observation (1968IV/1969I). This pattern recurs in the cusumsq plot, which in fact crosses the 5 per cent significance line and achieves its maximum deviation from the mean value line at the nineteenth observation (1968IV).

In order to pursue the possibility of a structural break in the German data we applied Quandt's log-likelihood ratio technique (Quandt, 1958, 1960). This is appropriate when an unknown switch point is hypothesized — the switch being characterized as an abrupt change from one constant regression relationship $(\beta^{(1)}, \sigma_1^2)$ to another $(\beta^{(2)}, \sigma_1^2)$.

For each t from $t = k + 1$ (1965II) to $t = T - k - 1$ (1970II), we computed and plotted:

$$\lambda_t = \log_{10} \frac{(\text{max likelihood given H}_0)}{(\text{max likelihood given H}_1)} \qquad (5.10)$$

Figure 5.1 UK cusum plot

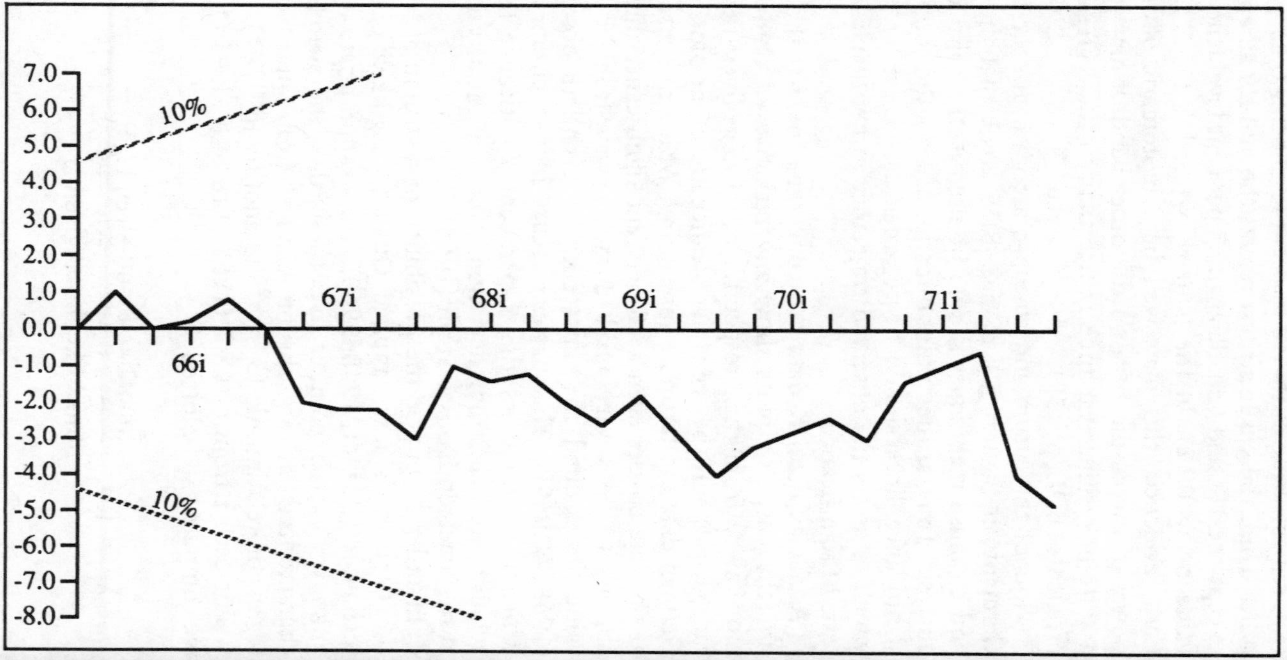

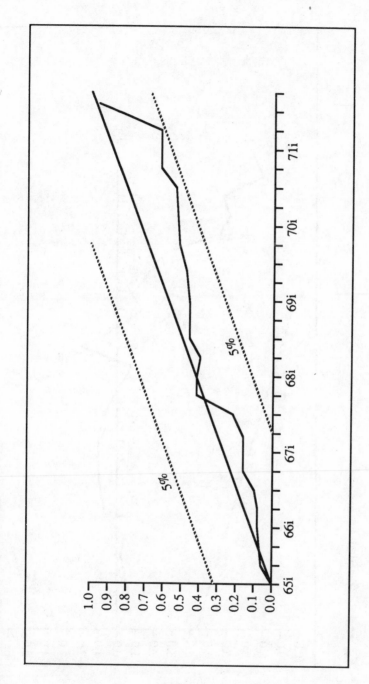

Figure 5.2 UK casualty plot

141

Figure 5.3   German cusum plot

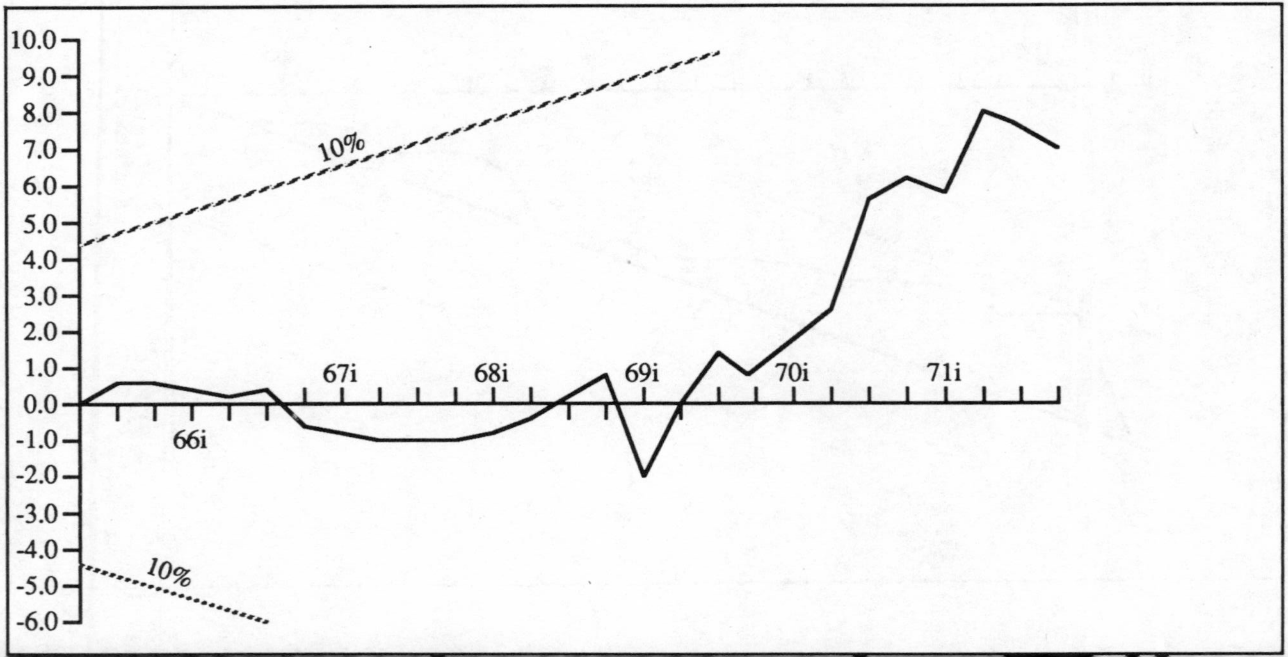

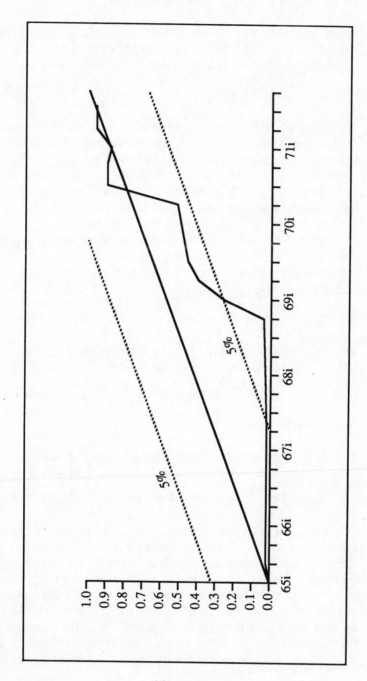

Figure 5.4 German cusumsq plot

143

where H_1 is the hypothesis that the observations in the time segments $(1, t)$ and $(t + 1, T)$ are the product of two different data-generating processes. It is easy to show:

$$\lambda_t = t \log \hat{\sigma}_1^2 + (T-t)\log \hat{\sigma}_2^2 - T \log \hat{\sigma}^2 \qquad (5.11)$$

where $\hat{\sigma}_1^2$, $\hat{\sigma}_2^2$ and $\hat{\sigma}^2$ are the ratios of residual sums of squares to number of observations when the regression is fitted to the first t, remaining $(T-t)$ and the whole set of observations respectively. The distribution of min λ_t is in fact unknown, but examining the behaviour of λ_t visually may shed some light on the location of the hypothesized switch point.

Quandt's λ_t, calculated using the German data, is graphed in Figure 5.5, which clearly indicates an abrupt change in the German data after the fourth quarter of 1968 (observation 19). Splitting the data into two sets at 1968IV and re-estimating the German equation we obtained:

(a) 1964II–1968IV

$$\hat{R} = 1.18 - 0.0003\hat{D} + 0.027\hat{y} + 4.43\,CAB/Y - 2.76\dot{d}$$
$$\quad\;(0.66)\,(0.0002)\quad(0.430)\quad(1.16)\qquad(1.23)$$

$$R^2 = 0.58;\; \bar{R}^2 = 0.46;\; DW = 1.71;\; SER = 2.04;\; T = 19.$$

(b) 1969I–1971IV

$$\hat{R} = 6.86 - 0.13\hat{D} + 3.90\hat{y} + 1.68\,CAB/Y - 4.56\dot{d}$$
$$\quad\;(4.58)\,(0.03)\quad(2.22)\quad(2.42)\qquad(4.46)$$

$$R^2 = 0.83;\; \bar{R}^2 = 0.74;\; DW = 2.03;\; SER = 10.25;\; T = 12.$$

Clearly, no tests can be carried out for the equality of co-efficients over the period since they would be subject to pre-test bias. Nevertheless, a casual examination of the two regression results does suggest a shift in both regression parameters and residual variance after 1968. This corresponds exactly with the franc/mark crisis of 1968–9. The sharp upward shift in the estimated value of the offset coefficient thus corresponds to a known increase in capital flows, even though the data have been adjusted for speculative capital

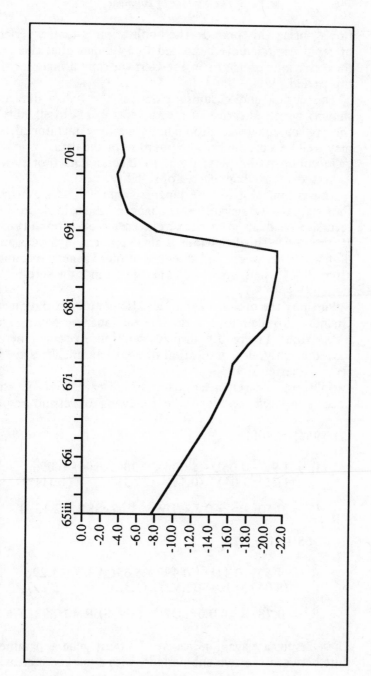

Figure 5.5   Plot of Quandt's log-likelihood ratio for German data

flows during this period. The implication is that experience of rapid capital movements led to a fundamental change in the behaviour of agents in the German capital markets after this period.

The cusum and cusumsq plots for the Italian data (not shown) were indicative of a very general lack of stability in the Italian equation, although, as we have mentioned, this may well be a product of the poorness of the data.

In contrast, the plots for the Canadian data (not shown) indicated a fairly high degree of stability.

The cusum plot for the Japanese data indicates a marked (but statistically insignificant) change in the behaviour of the recursive residuals after the seventeenth observation (1969II) (Figure 5.6). This behaviour is also apparent in the cusumsq plot which, however, indicates rather more general instability after 1968II than would be expected from a discrete regime switch (Figure 5.7).

Pursuing the matter further, we also computed and plotted Quandt's log-likelihood ratio for the Japanese data (Figure 5.8). Whilst Figure 5.8 displays multiple extrema, there is indeed a fairly clear indication of a structural shift after the second quarter of 1968.

Splitting the Japanese data set after the seventeenth observation, we obtained the following regression results:

(a) 1964II–1968II

$$\hat{R} = \begin{matrix} 1.92 \\ (1.26) \end{matrix} - \begin{matrix} 0.06\hat{D} \\ (0.04) \end{matrix} + \begin{matrix} 1.00\hat{y} \\ (0.45) \end{matrix} + \begin{matrix} 2.38\text{CAB/Y} \\ (2.65) \end{matrix} - \begin{matrix} 0.09\dot{d} \\ (1.51) \end{matrix}$$

$$R^2 = 0.50; \ \bar{R}^2 = 0.34; \ DW = 1.67; \ SER = 2.13; \ T = 17.$$

(b) 1968III–1971IV

$$\hat{R} = \begin{matrix} -4.55 \\ (8.04) \end{matrix} - \begin{matrix} 0.41\hat{D} \\ (0.10) \end{matrix} + \begin{matrix} 0.49\hat{y} \\ (1.92) \end{matrix} + \begin{matrix} 5.69\text{CAB/Y} \\ (1.38) \end{matrix} - \begin{matrix} 3.29\dot{d} \\ (5.29) \end{matrix}$$

$$R^2 = 0.78; \ \bar{R}^2 = 0.68; \ DW = 1.89; \ SER = 10.92; \ T = 14.$$

These results are again indicative of a fairly general parameter shift between the two sub-periods, with a marked increase in

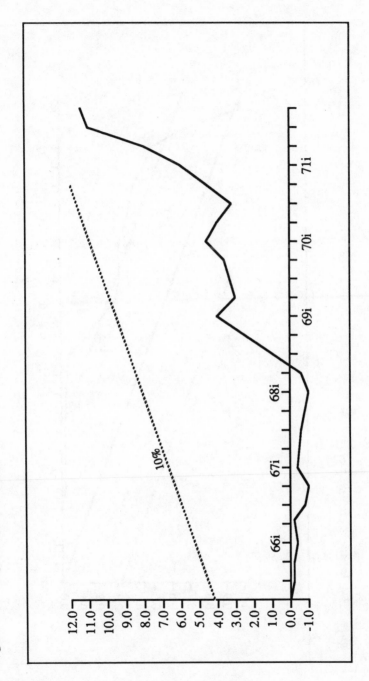

Figure 5.6 Japanese cusum plot

147

Figure 5.7 Japanese cusumsq plot

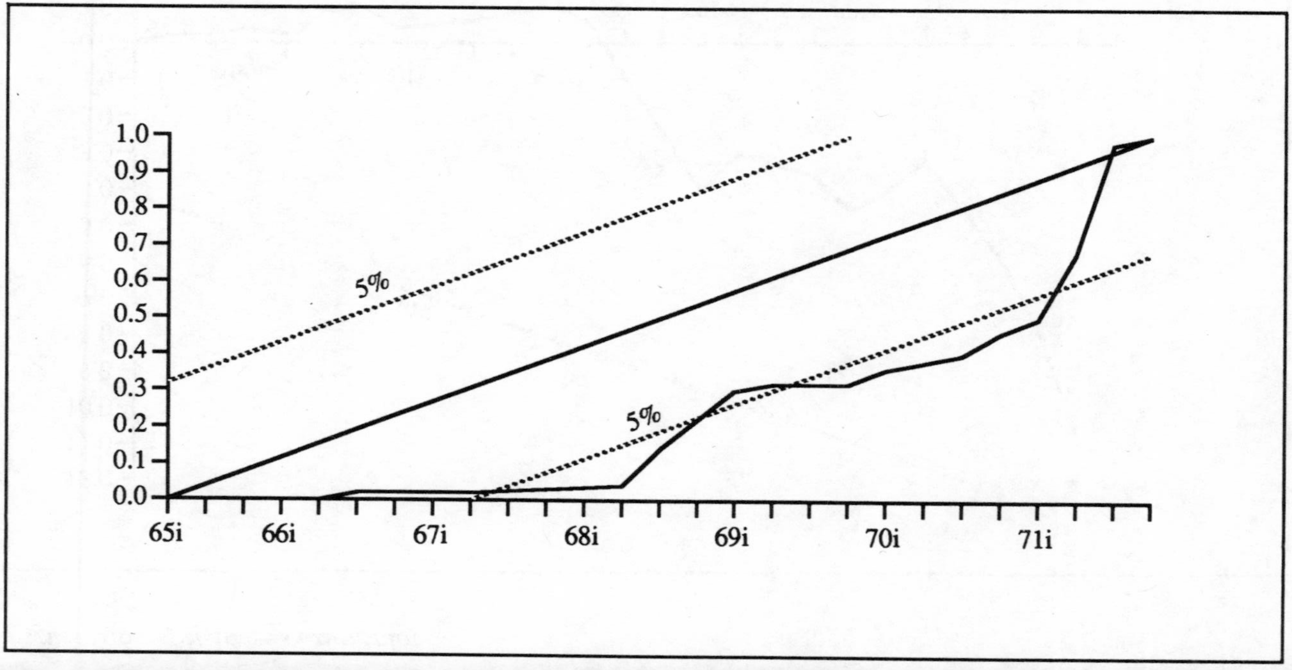

148

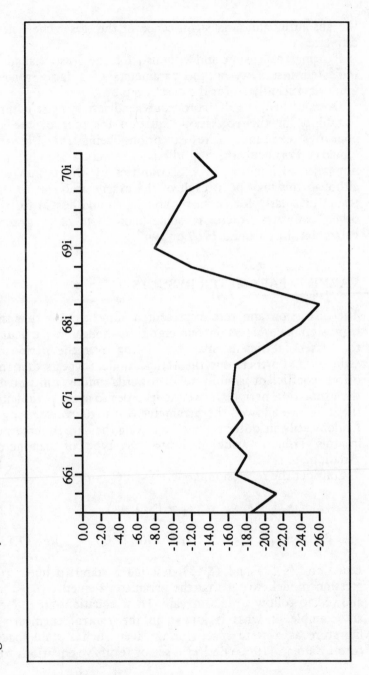

Figure 5.8 Plot of Quandt's log-likelihood ratio for Japanese data

the absolute value and significance of the offset coefficient estimate.

Plotting the cusum and cusumsq for the Australian data indicated instability in the parameters of a fairly general kind, significantly so for the cusumsq plot.

Overall, then, the BDE procedures indicate some structural instability in the regression equation for four of the six countries examined (the exceptions being the UK and Canada). Formally, the hypothesis of structural stability was not rejected for any of the countries by the cusum test although this may be a result of the exaggerated size of this test. Particularly for Germany and Japan and less so for the other countries, there is some indication of a general parameter shift around 1967 or 1968.

VARYING–PARAMETER RESULTS

The discussion and results presented above suggest that the regression parameters in our empirical model, in particular the offset coefficient, may be varying over the period of estimation. Further, our theoretical model suggests that the offset coefficient should tend towards minus unity over the estimation period. However, in order to avoid prejudging the issue, we allowed the parameter vector to evolve along a random walk in order to see if allowing the data to 'breathe' in this fashion would indicate the type of parameter variation.

Consider the regression model:

$$y_t = x_t'\beta_t + \epsilon_t \qquad \epsilon_t \sim IN(0, \sigma^2) \qquad (5.12)$$

$$\beta_t = \beta_{t-1} + \pi_t \qquad \pi_t \sim IN(0, \sigma^2 Q) \qquad (5.13)$$

Equations (5.12) and (5.13) describe a standard linear regression model except that the parameter sequence $\{\beta_t\}_1^T$ is allowed to follow a random walk. These equations are in fact an example of what is known in the control engineering literature as a state space form. Given such a state space form, Kalman (1960) derives a set of recursive equations for obtaining optimal estimates of the unknown vector sequence, known as the Kalman filter. Given the complete data set, estimates of the parameter sequence can be constructed which utilize all of the sample information, and these are termed 'smoothed' estimates. If Q is in fact a null matrix, then the Kalman filter, in this application, reduces to recursive least squares. A full description of the Kalman filter may be found in Anderson and Moore, 1979, and in a form amenable to econometricians in Harvey, 1981. Since σ^2 and Q are unknown, they must in fact be estimated and Harvey (1981) discusses how this may be done by maximum likelihood methods. In our estimations Q was taken to be diagonal. A brief discussion of the Kalman filter recursions and maximum likelihood estimation of the state space form is given in Appendix 5.3, whilst Appendix 5.4 lists the FORTRAN program used in the estimations reported below.

The diagonal elements of $Q = [q_{ii}]$ and σ^2 were estimated for the UK as:

$$\tilde{q}_{ii} = \begin{cases} 0.0040, & i = 1 \\ 0.0004, & i = 2 \\ 0.0000, & i = 0, 3, 4 \end{cases}$$

$$\tilde{\sigma}^2 = 14.79$$

Only the coefficients of the domestic credit and income variables were time-varying and the variance of the latter was only a tenth of that of the former.

Smoothed estimates of the vector sequence $\{\beta_i\}_1^T$ were then computed and are reported in Tables 5.3 and 5.4.

As the tables reveal, our priors (5.2) are again easily satisfied. What is more interesting, however, is that the smoothed estimates, in particular of the offset coefficient, are not really as we should expect them to be if they were in fact generated by a random walk; Figure 5.9 plots the smoothed estimates of the offset coefficient for the UK data. Given the relatively small variation in the coefficient of $\hat{y}$, the implication is that the primary source of parameter variation was probably an upward trend in international capital mobility as reflected in the offset coefficient.

Table 5.3   UK constant coefficients results

Const.	CAB/Y	$\dot{d}$
3.45	1.12	−0.84
(2.08)	(0.55)	(0.38)

Table 5.4   UK random walk coefficients results

Time	$\hat{D}$	$\hat{y}$	Time	$\hat{D}$	$\hat{y}$
1965iii	−0.32 (0.08)	1.13 (0.54)	1968iv	−0.72 (0.15)	0.93 (0.30)
1965iv	−0.32 (0.08)	1.13 (0.46)	1969i	−0.73 (0.15)	0.86 (0.32)
1966i	−0.42 (0.08)	1.20 (0.38)	1969ii	−0.74 (0.15)	0.87 (0.45)
1966ii	−0.46 (0.12)	1.01 (0.35)	1969iii	−0.77 (0.15)	0.88 (0.46)
1966iii	−0.49 (0.12)	1.52 (0.35)	1969iv	−0.82 (0.15)	0.80 (0.45)
1966iv	−0.53 (0.12)	1.39 (0.35)	1970i	−0.89 (0.15)	0.87 (0.32)
1967i	−0.56 (0.12)	1.10 (0.35)	1970ii	−0.93 (0.15)	0.83 (0.42)
1967ii	−0.59 (0.15)	0.80 (0.31)	1970iii	−0.97 (0.15)	0.86 (0.44)
1967iii	−0.61 (0.15)	0.92 (0.30)	1970iv	−1.00 (0.15)	0.92 (0.48)
1967iv	−0.63 (0.15)	0.95 (0.35)	1971i	−1.03 (0.15)	0.99 (0.46)
1968i	−0.66 (0.15)	0.93 (0.35)	1971ii	−1.07 (0.15)	1.07 (0.46)
1968ii	−0.69 (0.15)	0.91 (0.35)	1971iii	−1.06 (0.15)	1.30 (0.46)
1968iii	−0.72 (0.15)	0.93 (0.38)	1971iv	−1.09 (0.19)	1.39 (0.49)

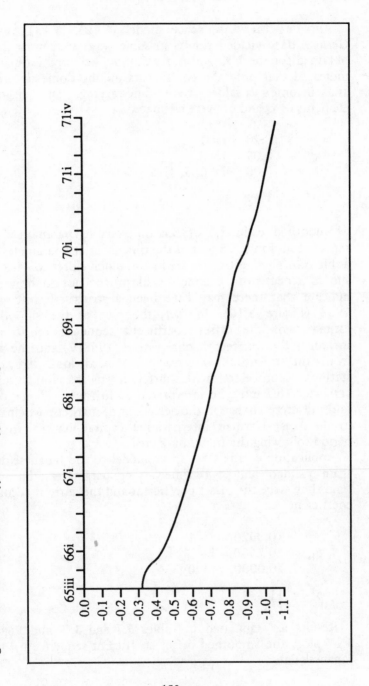

Figure 5.9   UK smoothed offset coefficient sequence

Applying the state space model (5.12), (5.13) to the German data yielded results in some ways similar to those obtained for the UK. Again, maximum likelihood estimation indicated that only the coefficients on the domestic credit and income variables were time-varying. The diagonal elements of Q and σ^2 were estimated as:

$$\tilde{q}_{ii} = \begin{cases} 0.20, & i = 1 \\ 0.09, & i = 2 \\ 0.00, & i = 0, 3, 4 \end{cases}$$

$$\tilde{\sigma}^2 = 1.09$$

Smoothed estimates of the time-varying parameters are reported in Table 5.5 and of the time-invariant parameters in Table 5.6. These estimates are in fact much closer to what we should expect from a random walk process but do, however, indicate that there may have been a structural shift after 1968 (Figure 5.10). In fact, the plot of the smoothed estimates of the offset coefficient sequence up to and including the nineteenth observation (1968IV) and the plot from the twentieth observation onward look like two stationary processes with different means but similar variance. This must be interpreted as further evidence of a fairly discrete change in the behaviour of market participants in the West German international capital markets in the period following the franc/mark crisis.

Application of the state space model to the Japanese data again yielded only two time-varying parameters, but this time they were the offset coefficient and the current account coefficient:

$$\tilde{q}_{ii} = \begin{cases} 0.0020, & i = 1 \\ 0.2580, & i = 3 \\ 0.0000, & i = 0, 2, 4 \end{cases}$$

$$\tilde{\sigma}^2 = 11.435$$

Results are tabulated in Tables 5.7 and 5.8, and Figure 5.11 plots the smoothed offset coefficient sequence for the Japanese data.

Table 5.5   *German constant coefficients results*

	Const.	CAB/Y	$\dot{d}$
	1.88 (1.81)	1.56 (0.69)	−0.43 (0.26)

Table 5.6   *German random walk coefficients results*

Time	$\hat{D}$	$\hat{y}$	Time	$\hat{D}$	$\hat{y}$
1965iii	−0.003 (0.022)	1.37 (0.94)	1968iv	−0.019 (0.053)	1.09 (0.72)
1965iv	−0.074 (0.007)	1.31 (0.91)	1969i	−0.769 (0.057)	1.25 (0.73)
1966i	−0.237 (0.014)	1.24 (0.88)	1969ii	−0.705 (0.109)	1.38 (0.71)
1966ii	−0.037 (0.014)	1.04 (0.89)	1969iii	−0.731 (0.121)	1.39 (0.69)
1966iii	−0.084 (0.021)	0.84 (0.88)	1969iv	−0.820 (0.148)	1.43 (0.64)
1966iv	−0.028 (0.013)	0.65 (0.86)	1970i	−0.802 (0.132)	1.48 (0.55)
1967i	−0.076 (0.062)	0.47 (0.87)	1970ii	−0.721 (0.186)	1.45 (0.43)
1967ii	−0.204 (0.009)	0.29 (0.86)	1970iii	−0.785 (0.185)	1.20 (0.58)
1967iii	−0.017 (0.054)	0.08 (0.84)	1970iv	−0.826 (0.182)	1.06 (0.69)
1967iv	−0.039 (0.051)	0.14 (0.81)	1971i	−0.874 (0.196)	1.06 (0.80)
1968i	−0.040 (0.042)	0.36 (0.77)	1971ii	−0.864 (0.191)	1.07 (0.89)
1968ii	−0.010 (0.014)	0.59 (0.71)	1971iii	−0.864 (0.197)	1.07 (0.97)
1968iii	−0.059 (0.010)	0.83 (0.71)	1971iv	−0.839 (0.195)	1.07 (1.01)

Figure 5.10   German smoothed offset coefficient sequence

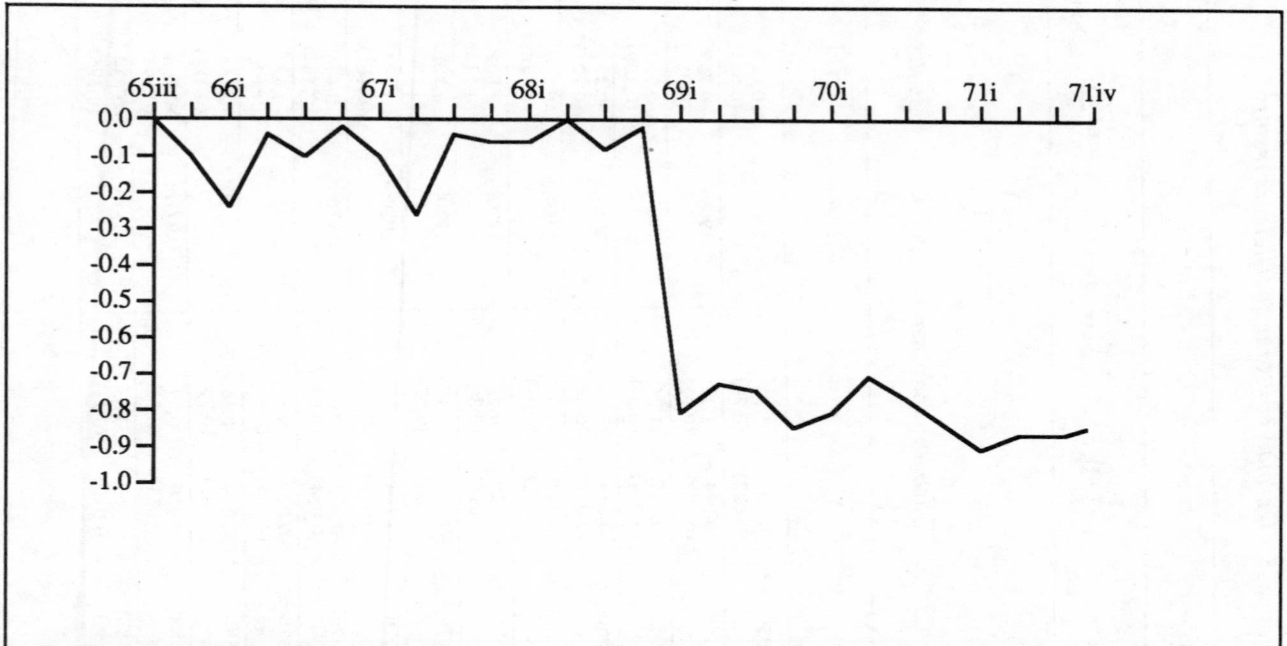

Table 5.7 Japanese constant coefficients results

Const.	$\hat{y}$	$\dot{d}$
2.42	0.75	−1.71
(1.60)	(0.41)	(1.03)

Table 5.8 Japanese random walk coefficients results

Time	$\hat{D}$	CAB/Y	*Time*	$\hat{D}$	CAB/Y
1965iii	0.038 (0.025)	2.18 (0.58)	1968iv	−0.024 (0.024)	4.18 (0.65)
1965iv	0.039 (0.024)	2.39 (0.63)	1969i	−0.062 (0.024)	3.49 (0.69)
1966i	0.026 (0.025)	2.34 (0.69)	1969ii	−0.087 (0.024)	2.69 (0.65)
1966ii	0.017 (0.025)	2.25 (0.66)	1969iii	−0.104 (0.023)	2.67 (0.62)
1966iii	0.006 (0.025)	2.22 (0.59)	1969iv	−0.122 (0.022)	3.07 (0.65)
1966iv	−0.003 (0.024)	2.53 (0.62)	1970i	−0.162 (0.022)	3.07 (0.71)
1967i	−0.007 (0.024)	2.95 (0.70)	1970ii	−0.186 (0.022)	3.01 (0.70)
1967ii	−0.012 (0.024)	3.38 (0.76)	1970iii	−0.209 (0.021)	3.25 (0.65)
1967iii	−0.016 (0.023)	3.76 (0.79)	1970iv	−0.235 (0.019)	4.30 (0.60)
1967iv	−0.019 (0.022)	4.20 (0.79)	1971i	−0.290 (0.018)	4.69 (0.59)
1968i	−0.024 (0.023)	4.64 (0.74)	1971ii	−0.335 (0.016)	4.93 (0.47)
1968ii	−0.027 (0.024)	4.24 (0.71)	1971iii	−0.381 (0.013)	5.24 (0.39)
1968iii	−0.028 (0.024)	4.94 (0.65)	1971iv	−0.401 (0.012)	5.01 (0.62)

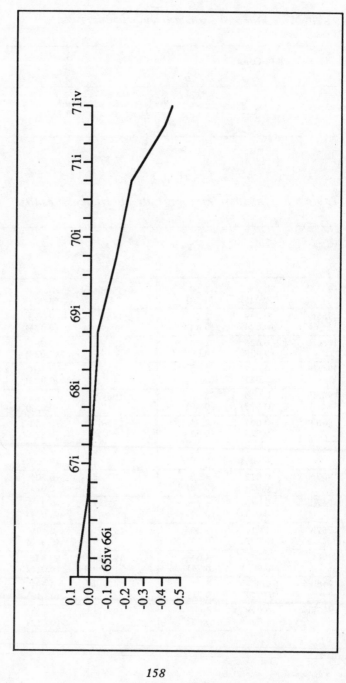

Figure 5.11   Japanese smoothed offset coefficient sequence

As can be seen from Figure 5.11, the smoothed estimates of the offset coefficient sequence again trend upward in absolute value and may again be indicative of a structural break after the fourth quarter of 1968 (observation 19). Since there does not appear to be any event specific to the yen around this period, this indication of an upward movement in capital mobility must be regarded as reflecting a global trend.

Applying maximum likelihood techniques to the state space model using Australian data yielded only one time-varying parameter — the offset coefficient:

$$\tilde{q}_{ii} = \begin{cases} 0.006, & i = 1 \\ 0.000, & i = 0, 2, 3, 4, \end{cases}$$

$$\tilde{\sigma}^2 = 2.92$$

See Tables 5.9 and 5.10, and Figure 5.12 for a plot of the smoothed offset coefficient sequence.

Examination of Figure 5.12 again suggests an upward trend in the absolute value of the offset coefficient, beginning markedly in the second quarter of 1968 and appearing to level off after the second quarter of 1970: further evidence of a global increase in capital mobility during this period.

When the state space model was applied to the Canadian data, maximum likelihood estimation failed to provide any indication of temporal variation in the parameters — Q was estimated as a null matrix. The estimate of σ^2 and smoothed estimates of the regression parameters were therefore identical to the OLS results reported in Table 5.1. This result may be interpreted as extremely strong evidence of the robustness of the Canadian equation over the sample period, particularly when considered together with the results of other methods applied above to the Canadian data. This suggests, in particular, that the Canadian and US markets were highly integrated for the whole of the 1960s.

Estimates obtained using the Italian data were extremely poor, with some elements of the estimated offset sequence lying outside the prior unit interval [–1, 0] and most co-efficients insignificantly different from zero. They are

Table 5.9   Australian constant coefficients results

Const.	$\hat{y}$	CAB/Y	$\dot{d}$
5.05	2.38	6.80	−3.14
(3.34)	(0.64)	(1.38)	(0.99)

Table 5.10   Australian random walk coefficients results

Time	$\hat{D}$	Time	$\hat{D}$
1965iii	−0.19 (0.06)	1968iv	−0.37 (0.06)
1965iv	−0.19 (0.06)	1969i	−0.41 (0.06)
1966i	−0.20 (0.05)	1969ii	−0.46 (0.05)
1966ii	−0.22 (0.04)	1969iii	−0.51 (0.05)
1966iii	−0.21 (0.05)	1969iv	−0.54 (0.05)
1966iv	−0.20 (0.05)	1970i	−0.58 (0.06)
1967i	−0.21 (0.06)	1970ii	−0.63 (0.06)
1967ii	−0.22 (0.06)	1970iii	−0.62 (0.06)
1967iii	−0.23 (0.06)	1970iv	−0.61 (0.06)
1967iv	−0.24 (0.06)	1971i	−0.61 (0.05)
1968i	−0.27 (0.06)	1971ii	−0.61 (0.04)
1968ii	−0.31 (0.06)	1971iii	−0.58 (0.06)
1968iii	−0.34 (0.06)	1971iv	−0.59 (0.07)

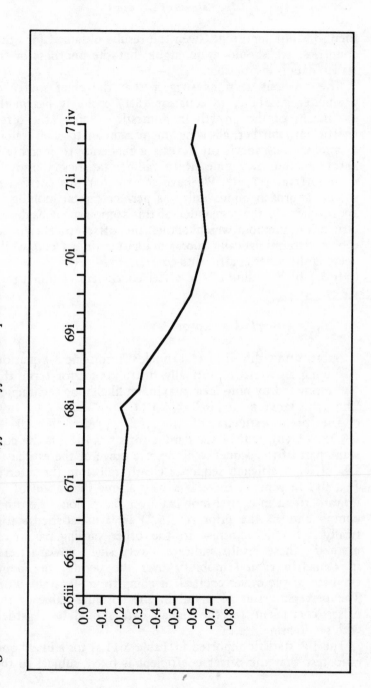

Figure 5.12 Australian smoothed offset coefficient sequence

therefore not reported. Given the results obtained for other countries, we should again argue that the poorness of the Italian data is responsible.

The previous sections suggest that the chief source of parameter instability in equation (5.1) probably lies in the coefficient of the growth in domestic credit — the offset coefficient. Further, allowing this parameter to evolve along a random walk inevitably reveals a tendency to increase in absolute value over time whilst falling statistically into the prior interval [-1, 0]. We have shown that this coefficient should approach minus unity as perfect capital mobility is approached. In the remainder of this section we consider an estimation method which allows the offset coefficient to evolve deterministically along a logistic time trend whilst keeping the other coefficients constant.

If β_{1t} be the value of the offset coefficient at time t then we can write:

$$\beta_{1t} = \beta + \gamma / \ 1 + \exp(\delta t)$$

Substituting this into (5.1) yields a non-linear equation. Assuming an additive, normally distributed error term, this was estimated by non-linear maximum likelihood techniques. The results are reported in Table 5.11.

The point estimate of $(\beta_{1,1}, \beta_{1,31})$ for the UK is (-0.39, -1.48); with a standard error of 0.461 on the constant part of the sequence alone, the range of the estimated UK offset coefficient sequence clearly falls into the interval [-1, 0]. In general, there is a very strong indication of an upward trend in capital mobility over the period. The other components of the prior set (5.2) are also satisfied statistically. Also, in contrast to the other varying parameter methods, these results indicate a very slight upward trend in Canadian capital mobility over the period, the point estimate of the offset coefficient going from -0.62 to -0.85. The perverse result of a fall in the absolute value of the offset coefficient for the Italian data should be regarded with scepticism.

The LR statistic reported in Table 5.11 is for a likelihood ratio test that the offset coefficient is fixed, subject to the

Table 5.11 Logistic trend offset coefficient model results

Country	Const.	β	γ	δ	β_{1_t} (t=1)	β_{1_t} (t=31)	$\dot{y}$	CAB/Y	$\dot{d}$	LR $\chi^2(2)$
UK	3.91 (1.51)	-11.333 (0.461)	21.958 (0.880)	0.0066484 (0.0021931)	-0.39	-1.48	1.27 (0.40)	0.88 (0.45)	-2.41 (1.91)	9.66
Germany	1.79 (1.84)	-2.753 (0.337)	5.387 (0.651)	0.0023678 (0.0012051)	-0.06	-0.16	2.14 (0.99)	3.14 (2.41)	-2.89 (2.15)	11.29
Italy	-0.53 (2.12)	-0.053 (0.072)	-2.963 (1.254)	2.1194000 (1.6792000)	-0.37	-0.05	0.22 (0.73)	5.31 (2.71)	-3.44 (1.92)	6.15
Canada	3.64 (1.71)	-0.852 (0.037)	0.554 (0.495)	0.3396800 (0.3257689)	-0.62	-0.85	0.10 (0.09)	5.15 (2.85)	-0.29 (0.18)	5.86
Japan	0.56 (3.40)	3.016 (0.374)	-6.262 (0.693)	-0.0056103 (0.0036870)	-0.12	-0.39	0.29 (0.17)	3.85 (0.61)	-3.76 (2.20)	8.31
Australia	6.47 (2.30)	-3.093 (1.031)	6.033 (0.751)	0.0112661 (0.0026900)	-0.09	-0.60	0.35 (0.18)	6.59 (2.51)	-1.72 (1.18)	9.47

maintained hypothesis that the other coefficients are fixed, and is computed by considering the logistic trend specification as the unrestricted form and the OLS model as the restricted form. Under the null hypothesis of no coefficient variation the statistic is asymptotically distributed as a central chi-square variate, with two degrees of freedom. As can be seen from the table, only the Canadian data accept the null hypothesis at the 5 per cent level, the critical value being 5.99. This result is fairly consistent with our earlier results and again indicates the high and sustained level of Canadian capital mobility, in contrast to the *growth* in capital mobility evidenced for the other countries.

CONCLUSION

In this chapter, we have applied a battery of statistical and econometric methods to the empirical portfolio balance model of balance of payments determination derived in Chapter 4. Overall, the portfolio balance approach model does, in fact, appear to fit the data quite well for the period examined, although, with the exception of the Canadian results, the (nested) pure monetary approach is not supported for the period as a whole.

Instantaneous (i.e. within quarter) sterilization does not appear to have been present, for the countries examined, in the 1960s except for the UK – probably through the operations of the Exchange Equalization Account. This is in contrast to the evidence of Obstfeld (1982) for West Germany for a similar period. However, we have questioned his econometric methods. This does not, however, deny the possibility that sterilization was present, but that except for the UK it does not appear to have important implications for OLS estimation of reserve-flow relationships.

Logically distinct from the question of whether or not the authorities attempt to sterilize (of which there is perhaps anecdotal evidence) is whether such attempts will or can be successful. This will in part depend on the degree of bond substitutability and hence capital mobility.

Various varying parameter estimation methods reveal quite

a lot of stability in the parameters of the empirical model except for the offset coefficient. The offset coefficient estimates tend to drift upward in absolute value over the period of the 1960s up to 1971. This indicates an increase in capital mobility over the period. We discussed the background to the period of estimation and suggested several factors which tended to increase the level of capital mobility during the 1960s. These included a rise in the level of international trade and consequent possibilities for leading and lagging payments; the rise of multinational corporations and opportunities to shift funds between subsidiaries (thereby avoiding exchange controls); and, thirdly, the growth and development of the international capital markets — notably the Eurodollar and Eurocurrency markets.

Further, there appears to be a sharp increase in the measured level of capital mobility after about 1968. This break more or less coincides with a number of exchange rate crises and the suspension of the London Gold Pool, even though the data were adjusted for these factors. (Moreover, the method of prior adjustment of the data cannot be responsible for these results since an upward trend is indicated for the period following, as well as during, the crisis periods.) One implication is that lessons learnt concerning the ease and speed of international capital market transactions during periods of intense currency speculation were never forgotten. On the other hand, a certain amount of causation must run the other way. As we noted above, the high level of international capital mobility prevailing at the end of the 1960s had not been foreseen when the adjustable peg system was designed at the Bretton Woods Conference, and was a major factor in its breakdown in the early 1970s.

Overall, the very simple model developed in Chapter 4 can be seen to have performed well when confronted with the data, and supplies quite a lot of information about this turbulent period.

APPENDIX 5.1   DATA SOURCES

All data are seasonally unadjusted and quarterly. With the exception of data on current account balances, all data were obtained from the IMF International Financial Statistics (IFS) data tape. Specific line numbers (with individual differences noted in parentheses) were as follows:

International Reserves (R)   — IFS line 11;

Domestic Credit (D)   — High-powered money (IFS line 14) minus R;

Real income (y)   — GDP, IFS line 99b.r: UK (99b.p), Italy, Australia;
GNP, IFS line 99a.r: Germany, Canada, Japan;

Nominal income (Y)   — GDP, IFS line 99b: UK, Italy, Australia; GNP, IFS line 99a: Germany, Canada, Japan;

Foreign interest rate (i^*)   — US Treasury Bill Rate, IFS line 60c, divided by four to convert to a quarterly basis;

Domestic inflation rate ($\dot{p}$)   — Computed as the quarterly rate of change of the implicit GDP or GNP deflator;

Data on current account balances (CAB) were obtained from various issues of the OECD Main Economic Indicators Historical Statistics.

APPENDIX 5.2   SPECULATIVE DUMMIES

Periods during which speculative capital flows were unusually heavy were identified and binary variables defined. The variables were then adjusted by regressing them individually on the appropriate dummies and using the retrieved residuals as the adjusted variable. The dummies were defined as follows (in parentheses we cite our sources in the identification of speculative periods):

UK: $D_1 = (1, 1964\text{iv}-1966\text{iii}$
  $(0, \text{otherwise}.$

  $D_2 = (1, 1967\text{ii}-1967\text{iv}$
  $(0, \text{otherwise}.$

  (Tew, 1970, pp. 261–5).

Germany: $D_1 = (1, 1968\text{iii}-1969\text{iii}$
  $(0, \text{otherwise}.$

  (Krause, 1970, pp. 564–6).

Italy: $D_1 = (1, 1963\text{iii}-1964\text{i}$
  $(0, \text{otherwise}.$

  (*The Banker*, April 1964, p. 205).

Canada: $D_1 = (1, 1968\text{i}-1970\text{ii}-1971\text{iv}$
  $(0, \text{otherwise}.$

  (Krause, 1970, pp. 558–61;
  Meier, 1974, pp. 78–85).

Japan: $D_1 = (1, 1971\text{i}-1971\text{iv}$
  $(0, \text{otherwise}.$

  (Patrick and Rosovsky, 1976,
  pp. 434–7).

Australia: $D_1 = (1, 1971\text{i}-1971\text{iv}$
  $(0, \text{otherwise}.$

  (Kouri and Porter, 1974, p. 456;
  Downing, 1973, p. 132).

In addition, a further dummy was included in each regression in order to take account of the dollar–gold crisis and suspension of the Gold Pool in 1968 (see Tew, 1970, pp. 254–5):

$$D = \begin{cases} 1, & 1967\text{iv}-1968\text{i} \\ 0, & \text{otherwise.} \end{cases}$$

(In order to avoid perfect multicollinearity, D was incorporated into D_2 for the UK and D_1 for Canada.)

APPENDIX 5.3   THE KALMAN FILTER

The Kalman filter is applicable to models which can be written in state space form. Consider the following:

$$y_t = z_t'\beta_t + \epsilon_t, \qquad t = 1, \ldots, T \qquad (A5.1)$$

$$\beta_t = M\beta_{t-1} + R\eta_t, \quad t = 1, \ldots T \qquad (A5.2)$$

where

$$\epsilon_t \sim IN(0, \sigma^2 h_t)$$

$$\eta_t \sim IN(0, \sigma^2 Q)$$

$\left\{ z_t \right\}_1^T$ is a sequence of (m × 1) known vectors, M and R are fixed matrices of order (m × m) and (m × g) respectively, $\left\{ h_t \right\}_1^T$ is a known sequence of scalars and Q is a fixed (g × g) matrix. The (m × 1) vector β_t is the unobservable state vector. The Kalman filter is designed to provide optimal estimates of $\left\{ \beta_t \right\}_1^T$. Equations (A5.1) and A5.2) together comprise a state space form. (A5.1) is the measurement equation, which shows how an observed series is related to the state vector. The transition equation, (A5.2), describes the dynamic evolution of the state vector.

Given knowledge of the parameters of the state space form, the Kalman filter recursions provide optimal estimates of β_t using either information up to time t-1 (the prediction equations), information up to time t (the updating equations), or the full sample information (the smoothing equations).

Suppose we have an optimal predictor of β_{t-1} using all information up to time t-1, and denote this b_{t-1}. Then the prediction equation giving the optimal estimator of β_t using information up to time t-1, denoted $b_{t/t-1}$, is

$$b_{t/t-1} = Mb_{t-1} \qquad (A5.3)$$

The covariance matrix of $b_{t/t-1}$ can be shown to be given by

$$P_{t/t-1} = M P_{t-1} M' + R Q R' \qquad \text{(A5.4)}$$

where P_{t-1} is the covariance matrix of b_{t-1}.

Equations (A5.3) and (A5.4) denote the prediction equations of the Kalman filter. The updating equations, which update these predictions in the light of information at time t, are given by equations (A5.5) and (A5.6):

$$b_t = b_{t/t-1} + P_{t/t-1} z_t (y_t - z_t' b_{t/t-1})/f_t \qquad \text{(A5.5)}$$

$$P_t = P_{t/t-1} - P_{t/t-1} z_t z_t' P_{t/t-1}/f_t \qquad \text{(A5.6)}$$

where $f_t = z_t' P_{t/t-1} z_t + h_t$.

Note the role played in (A5.5) by the prediction error $(y_t - z_t' b_{t/t-1})$. This innovation contains all the new information in y_t and is used to update $b_{t/t-1}$ via the Kalman gain. The Kalman gain is the (m × 1) vector $P_{t/t-1} z_{t/f_t}$ and it essentially decides what weight to assign to the innovation.

Given a finite sequence of observations $\left\{ y_t \right\}_1^T$, the only state vector estimator which utilizes all the available information is b_T. The smoothing equations, (A5.7) and (A5.8), describe optimal, full sample information estimators:

$$b_{t/T} = b_t + P_t^* (b_{t+1/T} - M b_t) \qquad \text{(A5.7)}$$

$$P_{t/T} = P_t + P_t^* (P_{t+1/T} - P_{t+1/t}) P_t^{*'} \qquad \text{(A5.8)}$$

where $P_t^* = P_t M P_{t+1/t}^{-1}$

and $b_{T/T} = b_T$; $P_{T/T} = P_T$.

Equations (A5.3)–(A5.8) describe the Kalman filter recursions (Kalman, 1960).

The significance of the Kalman filter for estimation of varying parameter econometric models can be appreciated by letting z_t denote the vector of observed explanatory variables, x_t say:

$$z_t = x_t, \text{ for all t.}$$

Letting R be an identity matrix, equations (A5.1), (A5.2) become

$$y_t = x_t'\beta_t + \epsilon_t \tag{A5.9}$$

$$\beta_t = M\beta_{t-1} + \eta_t \tag{A5.10}$$

which describes a regression model with time-varying, auto-regressive parameters. Setting M equal to an (m × m) identity matrix yields the random walk parameter regression model discussed in the chapter.

At first sight, it may appear that the Kalman filter is in general non-operational, since it requires that all parameters of the state space form be known, with the exception of σ^2. In fact, any or all of the state space parameters can in principle be estimated by maximum likelihood methods. A natural by-product of the Kalman filter recursions is a sequence of one-step-ahead prediction errors, $\left\{v_t\right\}_1^T$ defined by

$$v_t = y_t - z_t'b_{t/t-1}$$

Using a result due to Schweppe (1965), it turns out that the likelihood function for the sample can be written entirely in terms of these innovations and their variances (f_t):

$$(y_1, \ldots, y_T) = -\frac{T}{2}\ln 2\pi - \frac{T}{2}\ln\sigma^2 - \frac{1}{2}\sum_{t=1}^{T}\ln f_t$$
$$- \frac{1}{2}\sigma^{-2}\sum_{t=1}^{T}v_t^2/f_t \tag{A5.11}$$

The scale factor σ^2 may be concentrated out of (A5.11) by substituting:

$$\hat{\sigma}^2 = \frac{1}{T}\sum_{t=1}^{T}v_t^2/f_t$$

so that maximizing the likelihood function can be seen to be equivalent to minimizing the function:

$$F = T \ln \hat{\sigma}^2 + \sum_{t=1}^{T} \ln f_t \qquad (A5.12)$$

It only remains to find a suitable initialization of the filter, i.e. values for b_0 and P_0. Occasionally, one may be able to use the unconditional expectation of the state vector and its covariance matrix or by forming generalized least squares estimates of b_K and P_K (see Harvey, 1981). Alternatively, one might follow Harvey and Phillips (1979) by setting a 'diffuse prior' of $b_0 = 0$ and $P_0 = \mu I$, where μ is a very large number.

For further discussion of the Kalman filter see Anderson and Moore, 1979, or Harvey, 1981.

APPENDIX 5.4   A KALMAN FILTER PROGRAM
FOR THE RANDOM WALK COEFFICIENTS MODEL

This appendix contains a listing of a FORTRAN computer
program for estimating a regression model with random walk
coefficients, as described in Appendix 5.3. With minor
modifications, this program is identical to the one used to
obtain the empirical results reported above. It is designed
for use with a model with five independent variables, but
could easily be modified to take more or less. In order to
make the program useful to as wide an audience as possible,
we have converted it to single precision. The program makes
use of NAG algorithm EO4JAF. This is an 'easy to use'
algorithm, and more experienced users may wish to use NAG
algorithm EO4JBF instead. The program is reasonably well
annotated and the mnemonics for the quantities in question
correspond fairly closely to the notation used in Appendix
5.3. With further modification, the program could also be
used to estimate other Kalman filter models such as the
Harvey–Todd (1983) forecasting model. Researchers making
use of this program or a modified form of it are requested to
cite this monograph as their source.

```
C   KALMAN FILTER FOR RANDOM WALK
    COEFFICIENT MODEL

    REAL F
    INTEGER IBOUND,IFAIL,J,LIW,LW,N,NOUT
    REAL BL(5),BU(5),W(70),X(5)
    INTEGER IW(7)
    REAL Y(32),Z(32,5),XC(5),FC,B(5,32),P(5,5,32),
    PTT(5,5,32),
   -BBIGT(5,32),PBIGT(5,5,32),SEBIGT(5,5,32)
    INTEGER I,K
    COMMON/FIRST/ Y,Z,SGMHAT
    COMMON/SECOND/ P,PTT,B
    COMMON/THIRD/ BBIGT,PBIGT,SEBIGT
    DATA NOUT /6/
    DO 10 K=2,32
    READ(5,1000) Y(K), (Z(K,I),I=2,5)
```

```
 10   CONTINUE
      DO 20 K=2,32
      Z(K,1)=1.0
 20   CONTINUE
      WRITE(NOUT,99999)
      N=5
      DO 30 I=1,5
      X(I)=1.0
 30   CONTINUE
      X(5)=1.5
      IBOUND=2
      DO 40 I=1,5
      BL(I)=0.0
      BU(I)=1000000.0
 40   CONTINUE
      LIW=7
      LW=70
      IFAIL=1
      CALL EO4JAF(N,IBOUND,BL,BU,X,F,IW,LIW,W,
      LW,IFAIL)
      IF (IFAIL.NE.0) WRITE(NOUT, 99998) IFAIL
      IF (IFAIL.EQ.1) GOT TO 50
      WRITE(NOUT,99997) F
      WRITE(NOUT,99996) (X(J),J=1,N)
      WRITE(NOUT,99995) SGMHAT
      DO 60 I=1.5
      XC(I)=X(I)
 60   CONTINUE
      CALL FUNCT1 (N,XC,FC)
      WRITE(6,2000)
      DO 70 K=7,32
      WRITE(6,3000)(B(I,K),I=1,5)
 70   CONTINUE
      CALL SMOOTH
      WRITE(6,4000)
      DO 80 K=7,32
      WRITE(6,5000)(BBIGT(I,K),I=1,5)
      WRITE(6,6000)(SEBIGT(I,I,K),I=1,5)
 80   CONTINUE
 90   CONTINUE
```

```
99999   FORMAT(1H1, 'ESTQ PROGRAM RESULTS')
99998   FORMAT(1H0, 'ERROR EXIT TYPE', I3, '– SEE
        EO4JAF DOCUMENT')
99997   FORMAT(1H0, 'FUNCTION VALUE AT EXIT IS',
        F16.8)
99996   FORMAT(1H0, 'AT THE POINT –',5F16.8)
99995   FORMAT(1H0, 'ESTIMATED VALUE OF SIGMA',
        F16.8)
 1000   FORMAT(5(2X,F12,8))
 2000   FORMAT(1H1, 'RANDOM WALK COEFFICIENTS
        – KALMAN FILTER – RESULTS')
 3000   FORMAT(1H0, 5F16.8)
 4000   FORMAT(1H1, 'SMOOTHED ESTIMATES FOR
        RANDOM WALK MODEL')
 5000   FORMAT(1H0, 5F16.8)
 6000   FORMAT(1H,1X,5(3X,'(',F11.8,')'))
        END
        SUBROUTINE FUNCT1(N,XC,FC)
        INTEGER N
        REAL XC(N),FC
        INTEGER I,J,K
        REAL PTT(5,5,32),P(5,5,32),Q(5,5),Z(32,5),
        B(5,32),Y(32),
       -YTT(32),V(32),FV(32),ZP(5),SUM
        COMMON/FIRST/ Y,Z,SGMHAT
        COMMON/SECOND/ P,PTT,B
        DO 11 I=1,5
        DO 11 J=1,5
        Q(I,J)=0.0
    11  CONTINUE
        DO 1 I=1,5
        Q(I,I)=XC(I)
     1  CONTINUE
C
C       INITIALIZE THE KALMAN FILTER
C
        DO 2 I=1,5
        B(I,1)=0.0
     2  CONTINUE
        DO 3 I=1,5
```

```
         DO 3 J=1,5
         P(I,J,1)=0.0
   3     CONTINUE
         DO 4 I=1,5
         P(I,I,1)=1000000.0
   4     CONTINUE
         DO 80 K=2,32
C
C        PREDICTION EQUATION FOR
         ERROR VARIANCE
C
         DO 10 J=1,5
         DO 10 I=1,5
         K1=K-1
         PTT(I,J,K)=P(I,J,K1)+Q(I,J)
  10     CONTINUE
C
C        PREDICTION EQUATION FOR OBSERVATIONS
C
         SUM=0.0
         DO 20 I=1,5
         SUM=SUM+Z(K,I)*B(I,K1)
  20     CONTINUE
         YTT(K)=SUM
C
C        EQUATION FOR ONE-STEP-AHEAD PREDICTION
         ERROR
C
         V(K)=Y(K)-YTT(K)
C
C        ONE-STEP-AHEAD PREDICTION
         ERROR VARIANCE
C
         DO 40 K=1,5
         SUM=0.0
         DO 30 I=1,5
         SUM=SUM+Z(K,I)*PTT(I,J,K)
  30     CONTINUE
         ZP(J)=SUM
  40     CONTINUE
```

```
      SUM=0.0
      DO 50 I=1,5
      SUM=SUM+ZP(I)*P(K,I)
   50 CONTINUE
      FV(K)=SUM+1.0
C
C     UPDATING EQUATION FOR ERROR VARIANCE
C
      DO 60 I=1,5
      DO 60 J=1,5
      P(I,J,K)=PTT(I,J,K)-ZP(I)*ZP(J)/FV(K)
   60 CONTINUE
C
C     UPDATING  EQUATION  FOR  STATE  VECTOR
C
      DO 70 I=1,5
      B(I,K)=B(I,K1)+ZP(I)*V(K)/FV(K)
   70 CONTINUE
   80 CONTINUE
C
C     COMPUTE OBJECTIVE FUNCTION
C
      TOT=0.0
      SUM=0.0
      DO 90 I=7,32
      SUM=SUM+V(I)**2/FV(I)
      TOT=TOT+ALOG(FV(I))
   90 CONTINUE
      SGMHAT=SUM/ 26.0
      FC=ALOG(SGMHAT)+TOT/ 26.0
      RETURN
      END
      SUBROUTINE SMOOTH
      REAL PSTAR(5,5,32),P(5,5,32),PTT(5,5,32),
      PBIGT(5,5,32),TB(5,5)
     -INV(5,5),C(5,5),PST(5,5),DIFF(5,5),TRPST(5,5),
      PSTT(5,5),
     -PSTD(5,5),PSDPS(5,5),BDIFF(5,32),BBIGT(5,32),
      B(5,32),
     -PSTBD(5,32),SEBIGT(5,5,32)
```

```
          COMMON/SECOND/ P,PTT,B
          COMMON/THIRD/ BBIGT,PBIGT,SEBIGT
C
C         INITIALIZE THE SMOOTHING RECURSIONS
C
          DO 2 I=1,5
          BBIGT(I,32)=B(I,32)
          DO 1 J=1,5
          PBIGT(I,J,32)=P(I,J,32)
    1     CONTINUE
    2     CONTINUE
          DO 100 K=36,6,-1
          K1=K+1
C
C         SMOOTHING EQUATION FOR
          ERROR VARIANCE
C
          DO 10 I=1,5
          DO 10 J=1,5
          TB(I,J)=PTT(I,J,K1)
   10     CONTINUE
          CALL INVERT(TB,INV,K1)
          DO 20 I=1,5
          DO 20 J=1,5
          C(I,J)=P(I,J,K)
   20     CONTINUE
          CALL MMULT(C,INV,PST)
          DO 30 I=1,5
          DO 30 J=1,5
          PSTAR(I,J,K)=PST(I,J)
   30     CONTINUE
          DO 40 I=1,5
          DO 40 J=1,5
          DIFF(I,J)=PBIGT(I,J,K1)-PTT(I,J,K1)
          TRPST(I,J)=PSTAR(J,I,K)
          PSTT(I,J)=PSTAR(I,J,K)
   40     CONTINUE
          CALL MMULT(PSTT,DIFF,PSTD)
          CALL MMULT(PSTD,TRPST,PSDPS)
          DO 50 I=1,5
```

```
      DO 50 J=1,5
      PBIGT(I,J,K)=P(I,J,K)+PSDPS(I,J)
  50  CONTINUE
      DO 60 I=1,5
      SEBIGT(I,I,K1)=SQRT(PBIGT(I,I,K1))
  60  CONTINUE
C
C     SMOOTHING EQUATION FOR STATE VECTOR
C
      DO 70 I=1,5
      BDIFF(I,K)=BBIGT(I,K1)-B(I,K)
  70  CONTINUE
      DO 90 I=1,5
      SUM=0.0
      DO 80 J=1,5
      SUM=SUM+PSTAR(I,J,K)*BDIFF(J,K)
  80  CONTINUE
      BBIGT(I,K)=B(I,K)+SUM
  90  CONTINUE
 100  CONTINUE
      RETURN
      END
      SUBROUTINE MMULT(A,B,C)
      REAL A(5,5), B(5,5), C(5,5)
      DO 20 I=1,5
      DO 20 J=1,5
      SUM=0.0
      DO 10 J=1,5
      SUM=SUM+A(I,J)*B(J,K)
  10  CONTINUE
      C(I,K)=SUM
  20  CONTINUE
      RETURN
      END
      SUBROUTINE INVERT(A,C,K)
      REAL A(5,5), UNIT(5,5), WKSPCE(5)
      INTEGER I,N,J,IA,IUNIT,IFAIL
      REAL B(5,5), C(5,5)
      N=5
      IA=5
```

```
          IUNIT=5
          IFAIL=0
          CALL F01AAF(A,IA,N,UNIT,IUNIT,WKSPCE,
          IFAIL)
          DO 20 L=1,5
          DO 20 M=1,5
          C(L,M)=UNIT(L,M)
   20     CONTINUE
          IF(IFAIL.EQ.0) GO TO 30
          WRITE(6,10000) K
          WRITE(6,20000) ((B(L,M),L=1,5),M=1,5)
   30     RETURN
```

6. Conclusion

The balance of payments is a crucial topic in modern macro-economic analysis. At the policy level, the external constraint can impose severe restrictions on the choices open to policy-makers. Indeed, given the tremendously high level of capital mobility now obtaining in the international system, the external account can on occasion provide a means by which international capital market participants can discipline policy-makers — as witnessed, for example, by the failure of the Mitterrand experiment in France or by the international stock market crash of 1987 in the wake of the Louvre Accord (see Artis and Taylor, 1988).

This monograph started by examining the history of thought on the balance of payments since the seventeenth century. Over this period, we were able to discern three major shifts in emphasis. Firstly, we argued that the shift from the zero-sum analysis of the mercantilists to the harmonious systems of the classical economists essentially mirrored a shift in moral philosophy — from the selfish system of Hobbes (1651) to the reconciliation of public and private interest in Smith (1776).

The interwar period saw the influence of the Marginalist Revolution on balance of payments theory, with the develop-ment of the elasticities approach. We also discussed how the quantification afforded by the elasticities approach, together with early empirical demand studies, led to a mood of 'elasticity pessimism'. Other empirical work in this area suggested that the international payments system adjusted rather *too* rapidly after disturbances, and indicated that there may be other forces at work. The resolution of these paradoxes became only too obvious after the Keynesian Revolution.

The postwar period has seen a third shift in emphasis —

towards the monetary aspects of payments imbalance, and it is the monetary approach to the balance of payments which was taken as a starting point for the rest of our analysis.

Thus, in Chapter 2, we developed a fix-price general equilibrium model of a small open economy with tradeables, non-tradeables and an imported intermediate good. When the real side of the economy is allowed to clear continuously, the comparative statics of the model are identical to those of the monetary approach. In particular, both a devaluation and a pure increase in the money supply are long-run neutral. When the economy is stuck in a fix-price temporary equilibrium away from the Walrasian general equilibrium, however, the predictions of the model are quite different from those of the monetary approach. We also used this model to analyse the effects on the economy of an oil price shock.

The pure theory of Chapter 2 gave way to empirical analysis in Chapter 3, where we critically appraised some of the standard methods and results in the empirical literature on the monetary approach to the balance of payments. In particular, we showed that, contrary to conclusions which have been drawn by previous researchers, the presence or otherwise of Granger causality from the reserve variable to the domestic credit variable, in the standard MABP reserve-flow equation, can have no bearing on the relevant choice of econometric estimator. Secondly, we also showed how much of the previous, apparently supportive, empirical work on the MABP essentially reproduces a money stock identity in disguise. In particular, the estimated 'offset coefficient' in many previous studies, far from being an estimate of the reduced-form effect of the growth of domestic credit on the growth of international reserves, is in fact an estimate of minus unity.

In Chapter 4 we again turned to theoretical analysis. In particular, we developed a simple portfolio balance model of balance of payments adjustments which allows a varying level of international capital mobility and which nests the pure monetary approach (perfect capital mobility) as a special case. This resulted in a putative reduced form balance of payments equation which includes as explanatory variables the growth in the domestic component of the monetary base, the rate of growth of domestic real income, a proxy for the change in wealth and the change in the foreign interest rate adjusted for domestic inflation.

The estimated offset coefficient in this equation — showing the responsiveness of the balance of payments to changes in the level and growth of domestic credit — is itself an index of the level of international capital mobility. Thus, a zero offset coefficient would indicate zero capital mobility, whilst a value of minus unity would indicate perfect capital mobility. When the empirical portfolio balance model was estimated for a number of major OECD countries, using varying-parameter estimation techniques, the estimated offset coefficients tend to drift from very low negative levels towards minus unity over the period of the 1960s up to 1971. The major exception to this is the Canadian results, which indicate a fairly high and constant level of capital mobility between Canada and the US over the period. We have outlined in previous chapters the major reasons why there was such an apparent rise in international capital mobility during this period. Moreover, the results also tend to indicate a sharp rise in capital mobility after about 1968 — thus coinciding with a number of exchange rate crises and the suspension of the London Gold Pool, even though the data had been adjusted for these factors. We suggested in Chapter 5 that this may indicate that the high levels of international capital mobility concomitant with periods of intense currency speculation essentially became built into the system.

References

Aghelvi, B.B. and Khan, M.S. (1977), 'The Monetary Approach to Balance of Payments Determination: An Empirical Test', in *The Monetary Approach to the Balance of Payments*, International Monetary Fund, Washington, D.C.

Akhtar, M.A., Putnam, B.H. and Wilford, D.S. (1977), *Fiscal Constraints, Domestic Credit and International Reserve Flows*, mimeo, International Monetary Fund, Washington, D.C.

Alexander, S.S. (1952), 'Effects of a Devaluation on the Trade Balance', *International Monetary Fund Staff Papers*, 2, pp. 263–78.

Alexander, S.S. (1959), 'Effects of a Devaluation: A Simplified Synthesis of Elasticities and Absorption Approaches', *American Economic Review*, 49, pp. 23–42.

Allen, P.R. (1973), 'A Portfolio Approach to International Capital Flows', *Journal of International Economics*, 3, pp. 135–60.

Anderson, B.D.O. and Moore, J.B. (1979), *Optimal Filtering*, Englewood Cliffs, N.J.: Prentice-Hall.

Argy, V. (1977), 'Monetary Variables and the Balance of Payments', in *The Monetary Approach to the Balance of Payments*, Washington, D.C.: International Monetary Fund.

Argy, V. and Kouri, P.J.K. (1974), 'Sterilization Policies and the Volatility in International Reserves', in Aliber, R.Z. (ed.), *National Monetary Policies and the International Financial System*, Chicago: Chicago University Press.

Artis, M.J. and Taylor, M.P. (1988), 'Policy Coordination and Exchange Rate Stabilization', evidence submitted to the Treasury and Civil Service Committee, *International Monetary Coordination*, House of Commons.

Baillie, R.T., Lippens, R.E. and McMahon, P.C. (1983), 'Testing Rational Expectations and Efficiency in the Foreign Exchange Market', *Econometrica*, 51, pp. 553–63.

Balestra, P. and Nerlove, M. (1966), 'Pooling Cross-Section and Time Series Data in the Estimation of a Dynamic Model: The Demand for Natural Gas', *Econometrica*, 34, pp. 585–612.

Barnard, G.A. (1959), 'Control Charts and Stochastic Processes', *Journal of the Royal Statistical Society*, B, 21, pp. 239–71.

Barro, R.J. and Grossman, H.I. (1976), *Money, Employment and Inflation*, Cambridge: Cambridge University Press.

Bean, D.L. (1976), 'International Reserve Flows and Money Market Equilibrium: The Japanese Case', in Frenkel and Johnson (1976).

Begg, D.K.H. (1982), *The Rational Expectations Revolution in Macroeconomics*, Oxford: Philip Allan.

Bellman, R. (1960), *Introduction to Matrix Analysis*, New York: McGraw-Hill.

Belsley, D.A. (1973), 'The Applicability of the Kalman Filter in the Determination of Systematic Parameter Variation', *Annals of Economic and Social Measurement*, 4 (Special issue on Time-Varying Parameters), pp. 531–3.

Belsley, D.A. and Kuh, E. (1973), 'Time-Varying Parameter Structures: An Overview', *Annals of Economic and Social Measurement*, 4 (Special issue on Time-Varying Parameters), pp. 375–9.

Benjamin, D.K. and Kochin, L.A. (1979), 'Searching for an Explanation of Unemployment in Interwar Britain', *Journal of Political Economy*, 87, pp. 441–78.

Bennassy, J.P. (1975), 'Neo-Keynesian Disequilibrium Theory in a Monetary Economy', *Review of Economic Studies*, 62, pp. 503–24.

Berkeley, G. (1737), *Querist*, London.

Bickerdike, C.F. (1920), 'The Instability of Foreign Exchange', *Economic Journal*, 30, pp. 118–22.

Blejer, M.I. (1979), 'On Causality and the Monetary Approach to the Balance of Payments', *European Economic Review*, 12, pp. 289–96.

Borts, G.H. and Hansen, J.A. (1977), *The Monetary Approach to the Balance of Payments*, mimeo, Brown University, R.I.

Branson, W.H. (1968), *Financial Capital Flows in the US Balance of Payments*, Amsterdam: North Holland.

Branson, W.H. (1970), 'Monetary Policy and the New View of International Capital Movements', *Brookings Papers on Economic Activity*, 2, pp. 2355–62.

Branson, W.H. and Hill, R.D. (1971), 'Capital Movements Among Some Major OECD Countries: Some Preliminary Results', *The Journal of Finance*, 26, pp. 269–86.

Brems, H. (1957), 'Devaluation, a Marriage of the Elasticity and Absorption Approaches', *Economic Journal*, 67, pp. 49–64.

Breusch, T.S. and Pagan, A.R. (1979), 'A Simple Test for Heteroscedasticity and Random Coefficient Variation', *Econometrica*, 47, pp. 1287–94.

Brown, A.J. (1942), 'Trade Balances and Exchange Stability', *Oxford Economic Papers*, 6, pp. 57–76.

Brown, R.L., Durbin, J. and Evans, J.M. (1975), 'Techniques for Testing the Constancy of Regression Relationships over Time' (with discussion), *Journal of the Royal Statistical Society*, B, 37, pp. 149–92.

Bryant, R.C. and Hendershott, P.H. (1970), *Financial Capital Flows in the Balance of Payments of the United States: An Exploratory Empirical Study*, Princeton Studies in International Finance, No. 25, Princeton, N.J.: Princeton University International Finance Section.

Cagan, P. (1956), 'The Monetary Dynamics of Hyperinflation', in *Studies in the Quantity Theory of Money*, M. Friedman (ed.), Chicago: University of Chicago Press.

Caines, P.E. and Chan, V.W. (1975), 'Feedback between Stationary Processes', *IEEE Transactions on Automatic Control*.

Cantillon, R. (1755), *Essai sur la Nature du Commerce en Général*, Paris.

Chang, T.-C. (1946), 'The British Demand for Imports in the Inter-War Period', *Economic Journal*, 56, pp. 188–207.

Chow, G.C. (1960), 'Tests for Equality between Sets of Coefficients in Two Linear Regressions', *Econometrica*, 28, pp. 591–605.

Chow, G.C. (1984), *Econometrics*, New York: McGraw-Hill.

Clement, M.O., Pfister, R.L. and Rothwell, K.J. (1967), *Theoretical Issues in International Economics*, Boston.

Cobham, D. (1983), 'Reverse Causation in the Monetary Approach: An Econometric Test for the UK', *Manchester School*, 1983(4), pp. 360–79.

Connolly, M. and Taylor, D. (1976), 'Testing the Monetary Approach to Devaluation in Developing Countries', *Journal of Political Economy*, 84, pp. 849–59.

Cooley, T. (1971), *Estimation in the Presence of Sequential Parameter Variation*, doctoral thesis, University of Pennsylvania.

Cooley, T. and Prescott, E.C. (1973), 'Tests of an Adaptive Regression Model', *Review of Economics and Statistics*, 55, pp. 248–56.

Cooley, T. and Prescott, E.C. (1976), 'Estimation in the Presence of Stochastic Parameter Variation', *Econometrica*, 44, pp. 167–84.

Cox, W.M. and Wilford, D.S. (1977), *The Monetary Approach to the Balance of Payments and World Monetary Equilibrium*, mimeo, International Monetary Fund, Washington, D.C.

Cripps, F. and Godley, W. (1976), 'A Formal Analysis of the Cambridge Economic Policy Group Model', *Economica*, 43, pp. 335–48.

Cuddington, J.T. (1981), 'Money, Income and Causality in the United Kingdom', *Journal of Money, Credit and Banking*, 13, pp. 342–51.

Currie, D.A. (1976), 'Some Criticisms of the Monetary Analysis of Balance of Payments Correction', *Economic Journal*, 87, pp. 771–3.

Dent, W. and Geweke, J. (1979), *On Specification in Simultaneous Equations Models*, University of Wisconsin, Madison, Workshop Paper No. 7823.

Dixit, A.K. (1976), 'Public Finance in a Keynesian Temporary Equilibrium', *Journal of Economic Theory*, 12, pp. 242–58.

Dixit, A.K. (1978), 'The Balance of Trade in a Model of Temporary Equilibrium with Rationing', *Review of Economic Studies*, 45, pp. 393–404.

Dornbusch, R. (1973), 'Devaluation, Money and Non-Traded Goods', *American Economic Review*, 63, pp. 871–83.

Dornbusch, R. (1975), 'A Portfolio Balance Model of the Open Economy', *Journal of Monetary Economics*, 1, pp. 3–20.

Dornbusch, R. (1980), *Open Economy Macroeconomics*, New York: Basic Books.

Downing, R.I. (1973), *The Australian Economy*, London: Weidenfeld and Nicolson.

Einzig, P. (1937), *The Theory of Forward Exchange*, London: Macmillan.

Eliot, T.S. (1919), 'Tradition and the Individual Talent', published in *Egoist*, September and December.

Engle, R.F., Hendry, D.F. and Richard, J.F. (1983), 'Exogeneity', *Econometrica*, 51, pp. 277–304.

Enoch, C.A. (1979), *The Direction of Causality Between the Exchange Rate, Prices and Money*, Bank of England Discussion Paper No. 7.

Ezekial, M. (1941), *Methods of Correlation Analysis*, 2nd edition, New York: Wiley.

Feige, E.L. and Pearce, D.K. (1979), 'The Casual Causal Relationship Between Money and Income: Some Caveats for the Time Series Analysis', *Review of Economics and Statistics*, 56, pp. 521–33.

Fisk, P.R. (1967), 'Models of the Second Kind in Regression Analysis', *Journal of the Royal Statistical Society*, B, 28, pp. 266–81.

Frenkel, J.A. (1976), 'Adjustment Mechanisms and the Monetary Approach to the Balance of Payments: A Doctrinal Perspective', in *Recent Issues in International Monetary Economics*, Claasen, E.-M. and Salin, P. (eds), Amsterdam: North Holland.

Frenkel, J.A. (1980), 'Exchange Rates, Prices and Money: Lessons from the 1920s', *American Economic Review*, 70, pp. 235–42.

Frenkel, J.A. (1981), 'Flexible Exchange Rates, Prices and the Role of News: Lessons from the 1970s', *Journal of Political Economy*, 89, pp. 665–705.

Frenkel, J.A. and Johnson, H.G. (eds) (1976), *The Monetary*

Approach to the Balance of Payments, London: George Allen and Unwin.

Frenkel, J.A. and Johnson, H.G. (1976a), 'The Monetary Approach to the Balance of Payments: Essential Concepts and Historical Origins', in Frenkel and Johnson (1976).

Frenkel, J.A. and Johnson, H.G. (eds)(1978), *The Economics of Exchange Rates: Selected Studies*, London: Addison-Wesley.

Frenkel, J.A. and Rodriguez, C. (1975), 'Portfolio Equilibrium and the Balance of Payments: A Monetary Approach', *American Economic Review*, 65, pp. 674–88.

Frenkel, J.A., Gylfason, T. and Helliwell, J.F. (1980), 'A Synthesis of Monetary and Keynesian Approaches to Short-Run Balance-of-Payments Theory', *Economic Journal*, 90, pp. 582–92.

Friedman, M. (1953), *Essays in Positive Economics*, Chicago: Chicago University Press.

Garbade, K. (1977), 'Two Methods for Examining the Stability of Regression Coefficients', *Journal of the American Statistical Association*, 72, pp. 54–63.

Genberg, H. (1976), 'Aspects of the Monetary Approach to Balance of Payments Theory: An Empirical Study of Sweden', in Frenkel and Johnson (1976).

Gervaise, I. (1720), *The System or Theory of the Trade of the World*, London.

Geweke, J. (1978), 'Testing the Exogeneity Specification in the Complete Dynamic Simultaneous Equation Model', *Journal of Econometrics*, 7, pp. 163–85.

Geweke, J. (1982), 'Causality, Exogeneity and Inference', in Hildenbrand, W. (ed.), *Advances in Econometrics*, Cambridge: Cambridge University Press.

Godfrey, L.G. (1978), *A Diagnostic Check of the Variance Model in Regression Equations with Heteroscedastic Disturbances*, mimeo, University of York.

Goodhart, C.A.E. (1979), 'Money in an Open Economy', in Ormerod, P. (ed.), *Economic Modelling*, London: Heinemann.

Gossen, H.H. (1854), *Entwickelung der Gesetze des Menslichen Verkehrs, und der Daraus Fliessenden Regeln für Mensliches Handeln*, Brunswick.

Granger, C.W.J. (1969), 'Investigating Causal Relationships by Econometric Models and Cross-Spectral Methods', *Econometrica*, 37, pp. 424–38.

Grunfeld, Y. and Griliches, Z. (1960), 'Is Aggregation Necessarily Bad?', *Review of Economics and Statistics*, 42, pp. 1–13.

Gylfason, T. and Helliwell, J.F. (1983), 'A Synthesis of Keynesian, Monetary, and Portfolio Approaches to Flexible Exchange Rates', *Economic Journal*, 93, pp. 820–31.

Haberler, G. (1949), 'The Market for Foreign Exchange and the Stability of the Balance of Payments: A Theoretical Analysis', *Kyklos*, 3, pp. 193–218.

Hahn, F. (1959), 'The Balance of Payments in a Monetary Economy', *Review of Economic Studies*, 26, pp. 110–25.

Hansen, L.P. and Hodrick, R.J. (1981), 'Forward Exchange Rates as Optimal Predictors of Future Spot Rates: An Econometric Analysis', *Journal of Political Economy*, 88, pp. 829–53.

Harberger, A.C. (1950), 'Currency Depreciation, Income and the Balance of Trade', *Journal of Political Economy*, 58, pp. 47–60.

Harrod, R.F. (1939), *International Economics*, revised edition, London.

Harvey, A.C. (1981), *Time Series Methods*, Oxford: Philip Allan.

Harvey, A.C. and Phillips, G.D.A. (1979), 'The Estimation of Regression Models with Autoregressive-Moving Average Disturbances', *Biometrika*, 66, pp. 49–58.

Harvey, A.C. and Phillips, G.D.A. (1982), 'The Estimation of Regression Models with Time-Varying Parameters', in *Games, Economic Dynamics and Time Series Analysis*, Vienna: Physica-Verlag.

Hausman, J.A. (1978), 'Specification Tests in Econometrics', *Econometrica*, 46, pp. 1251–71.

Heckscher, E.F. (1931), *Mercantilism*, London: Macmillan (second edition 1955).

Henderson, J.M. and Quandt, R.E. (1980), *Microeconomic Theory: A Mathematical Approach*, third edition, New York: McGraw-Hill.

Hicks, J.R. (1937), 'Mr. Keynes and the Classics: A Suggested Interpretation', *Econometrica*, 5, pp. 147–59.

Hildreth, C. and Houck, J.P. (1968), 'Some Estimators for a Linear Model with Random Coefficients', *Journal of the American Statistical Association*, 63, pp. 584–95.

Hinshaw, R. (1945), 'American Prosperity and the British Balance of Payments Problem', *Review of Economics and Statistics*, 27, p. 4.

Hobbes, T. (1651), *Leviathan or the Matter, Form and Power of a Commonwealth, Ecclesiastical and Civil*, London.

Hodjera, Z. (1971), 'Short-Term Capital Movements of the United Kingdom, 1963–1967', *Journal of Political Economy*, 79, pp. 739–75.

Hume, D. (1751), *An Enquiry Concerning the Principles of Morals*, London.

Hume, D. (1752), 'Of the Balance of Trade', in *Essays, Moral, Political and Literary* (ed. D. Rotwein), London.

Hume, D. (1776), *An Enquiry Concerning Human Understanding*, London.

Hurwicz, L. (1950), 'Systems with Nonadditive Disturbances', in Koopmans, T.C. (ed.), *Statistical Inference in Dynamic Economic Models*, New York: Wiley.

Johannes, J.M. (1981), 'Testing the Exogeneity Specification Underlying the Monetary Approach to the Balance of Payments', *Review of Economics and Statistics*, 63, pp. 29–34.

Johnson, H.G. (1956), 'The Transfer Problem and Exchange Stability', *Journal of Political Economy*, 54, pp. 212–25.

Johnson, H.G. (1958), 'Towards a General Theory of the Balance of Payments', in his *International Trade and Economic Growth*, London: George Allen and Unwin.

Johnson, H.G. (1972), 'The Monetary Approach to Balance of Payments Theory', *Journal of Financial and Quantitative Analysis*, 7, pp. 220–74.

Johnson, H.G. (1976), 'The Monetary Approach to Balance of Payments Theory', in Frenkel and Johnson (1976).

Johnson, H.G. (1977), *Money, Balance-of-Payments Theory, and the International Monetary Problem*, Essays in International Finance No. 124, Princeton, N.J.: Princeton University International Finance Section.

Jong, F.J. de (1973), *Developments of Monetary Theory in the Netherlands*, Rotterdam: Rotterdam University Press.

Kaldor, N. (1983), *The Economic Consequences of Mrs Thatcher*, Fabian Tract No. 486, London: Fabian Society.

Kalman, R.E. (1960), 'A New Approach to Linear Filtering and Prediction Problems', *Journal of Basic Engineering*, D, 82, pp. 35–45.

Kant, I. (1790), *Kritik der Urtheilskraft*, Berlin: S.N.

Kemp, M.C. (1962), 'The Rate of Exchange, the Terms of Trade and the Balance of Payments in Fully Employed Economics', *International Economic Review*, 3, pp. 314–27.

Keynes, J.M. (1936), *The General Theory of Employment, Interest and Money*, London: Macmillan.

Klein, L.R. (1953), *A Textbook of Econometrics*, Evanston: Row Peterson.

Kmenta, J. and Gilbert, R.F. (1968), 'Small Sample Properties of Alternative Estimators of Seemingly Unrelated Regressions', *Journal of the American Statistical Association*, 63, pp. 1180–1200.

Komiya, R. (1969), 'Economic Growth and the Balance of Payments: A Monetary Approach', *Journal of Political Economy*, 77, pp. 35–48.

Koopmans, T.C. (1950), 'When is an Equation Complete for Statistical Purposes?', in Koopmans, T.C. (ed.), *Statistical Inference in Dynamic Economic Models*, New York: J. Wiley and Sons.

Koopmans, T.C. and Hood, W.C. (1953), 'The Estimation of Simultaneous Linear Economic Relationships', in Hood, W.C. and Koopmans, T.C. (eds), *Studies in Econometric Method*, New Haven, Conn.: Yale University Press.

Kouri, P.J.K. and Porter, M.G. (1974), 'International Capital Flows and Portfolio Equilibrium', *Journal of Political Economy*, 82, pp. 443–67.

Krause, L.B. (1970), 'Recent International Monetary Crises: Causes and Cures', in Smith, W.L. and Teiger, R.L. (eds), *Readings in Money, National Income, and Stabilization Policy*, revised edition, Homewood, Ill.: Richard Irwin.

Kreinin, M.E. and Officer, L.H. (1978), *The Monetary Approach to the Balance of Payments: A Survey*, Princeton Studies in International Finance, No. 43, Princeton, N.J.: Princeton University International Finance Section.

Krueger, A.V. (1969), 'Balance of Payments Theory', *Journal of Economic Literature*, 1, pp. 1–26.

Kuhn, T.S. (1970), *The Structure of Scientific Revolutions*, Chicago: University of Chicago Press.

Laidler, D.E.W. (1972), *Price and Output Fluctuations in an Open Economy*, University of Manchester Discussion Paper No. 7301.

Laursen, S. and Metzler, L. (1950), 'Flexible Exchange Rates and the Theory of Employment', *Review of Economics and Statistics*, 32, pp. 281–99.

Law, J. (1705), *Money and Trade Considered*, Edinburgh.

Leamer, E.E. (1978), *Specification Searches: Ad Hoc Inference with Non-Experimental Data*, New York: Wiley.

Lee, C.H. (1969), 'A Stock-Adjustment Analysis of Capital Movements', *Kyklos*, 23, pp. 65–74.

Leontief, W. (1947), 'Introduction to a Theory of the Internal Structure of Functional Relationships', *Econometrica*, 15, pp. 361–73.

Liviatan, N. (1963), 'Tests of the Permanent Income Hypothesis Based on a Re-Interview Savings Study', in Christ, C. (ed.), *Measurement in Economics*, Stanford: Stanford University Press.

Locke, J. (1690), *Two Treaties of Civil Government*, London.

Locke, J. (1691), 'Some Considerations of the Consequences of the Lowering of Interest, and Raising the Value of Money', in his *Several Papers Relating to Money, Interest and Trade*, London.

Lucas, R.E. (1976), 'Econometric Policy Evaluation: A Critique', in Brunner, K. and Meltzer, A.H. (eds), *The Phillips Curve and Labor Markets*, Carnegie–Rochester Conference Series No. 1, New York: North-Holland.

McCloskey, D.M. (1983), 'The Rhetoric of Economics', *Journal of Economic Literature*, 21, pp. 481–517.

McCulloch, J.H. (1975), 'Risk, Interest and Forward Exchange: Comment', *Quarterly Journal of Economics*, 89, pp. 170–2.

McFadden, D.L. (1978), 'Cost, Revenue and Profit Functions', in Fuss, M. and McFadden, D. (eds), *Production Economics: A Dual Approach in Theory and Applications*, Amsterdam: North-Holland.

Machlup, F. (1955), 'Relative Prices and Aggregate Spending in the Analysis of Devaluation', *American Economic Review*, 45, pp. 225–78.

Machlup, F. (1956), 'The Terms-of-Trade Effects of Devaluation upon Real Income and the Balance of Trade', *Kyklos*, 3, pp. 417–50.

McKinnon, R.I. (1969), 'Portfolio Balance and International Payments Adjustment', in Mundell, R.A. and Swoboda, A.K. (eds), *Monetary Problems of the International Economy*, Chicago: Chicago University Press.

McKinnon, R.I. and Oates, W.E. (1966), *The Implications of International Economic Integration for Monetary, Fiscal and Exchange Rate Policy*, Princeton Studies in International Finance, No. 16, Princeton, N.J.: Princeton University International Finance Section.

Magee, S.P. (1976), 'The Empirical Evidence on the Monetary Approach to the Balance of Payments and Exchange Rates', *American Economic Review*, 66, pp. 163–70.

Magnus, J.R. (1978), 'Maximum Likelihood Estimation of the GLS Model with Unknown Parameters in the Disturbance Covariance Matrix', *Journal of Econometrics*, 7, pp. 281–312.

Malinvaud, E. (1977), *The Theory of Unemployment Reconsidered*, Oxford: Basil Blackwell.

Mann, H.B. and Wald, A. (1943), 'On the Statistical Treatment of Linear Stochastic Difference Equations', *Econometrica*, 11, pp. 173–220.

Markowitz, H.M. (1959), *Portfolio Selection: Efficient Diversification of Investments*, New York: Wiley.

Marx, K. (1963), *Theories of Surplus Value*, London: Lawrence and Wishart.

Meade, J.E. (1952), *The Theory of International Economic Policy, Volume I: The Balance of Payments*, Oxford: Oxford University Press.

Meier, G.M. (1974), *Problems of a World Monetary Order*, New York: Oxford University Press.

Metcalf, D., Nickell, S.J. and Floros, N. (1982), 'Still Searching for an Explanation of Unemployment in Interwar Britain', *Journal of Political Economy*, 90, pp. 386-99.

Metzler, L.A. (1948), 'The Theory of International Trade', in Ellis, H.S. (ed.), *A Survey of Contemporary Economics*, Homewood, Ill.: Irwin.

Michaely, M. (1960), 'Relative-Prices and Income-Absorption Approaches to Devaluation: A Partial Reconciliation', *American Economic Review*, 9, pp. 218-27.

Mill, J.S. (1848), *Principles of Political Economy*, London (references to *Collected Works of John Stuart Mill*, Robson, J.M. (ed.), (1965), London).

Miller, N.C. and Whitman, M.V.N. (1970), 'A Mean-Variance Analysis of United States Long-Term Portfolio Foreign Investment', *Quarterly Journal of Economics*, 84, pp. 175-96.

Muellbauer, J. and Portes, R.D. (1978), 'Macroeconomic Models with Quantity Rationing', *Economic Journal*, 88, pp. 393-404.

Mun, T. (1664), *England's Treasure by Forraign Trade, or the Ballance of our Forraign Trade is the Rule of Our Treasure*, London.

Mundell, R.A. (1962), 'The Appropriate Use of Monetary and Fiscal Policies for Internal and External Stability', *International Monetary Fund Staff Papers*, 9, pp. 70-7.

Mundell, R.A. (1963), 'Capital Mobility and Stabilization Policy under Fixed and Flexible Exchange Rates', *Canadian Journal of Economics and Political Science*, 29, pp. 475-85.

Mundell, R.A. (1968), *International Economics*, New York: Macmillan.

Mundell, R.A. (1971), *Monetary Theory*, California: Goodyear.

Mundlak, Y. (1963), 'Estimation of Production and Behavioural Functions from a Combination of Cross-Section and Time Series Data', in Christ, C.F. (ed.), *Measurement in Economics*, Stanford: Stanford University Press.

Mussa, M. (1974), 'A Monetary Approach to Balance of Payments Analysis', *Journal of Money, Credit and Banking*, 6, pp. 333–51.

Neary, J.P. (1980), 'Nontraded Goods and the Balance of Trade in a Neo-Keynesian Temporary Equilibrium', *Quarterly Journal of Economics*, 94, pp. 403–29.

Neary, J.P. and Roberts, K.W.S. (1980), 'The Theory of Household Behaviour Under Rationing', *European Economic Review*, 13, pp. 25–42.

Neary, J.P. and Stiglitz, J.E. (1983), 'Towards a Reconstruction of Keynesian Economics: Expectations and Constrained Equilibria', *Quarterly Journal of Economics*, 98, pp. 199–228.

Negishi, T. (1968), 'Approaches to the Analysis of Devaluation', *International Economic Review*, 9, pp. 218–27.

Nerlove, M. (1965), *Estimation and Identification of Cobb-Douglas Production Functions*, Chicago: Rand McNally.

Nobay, A.R. and Johnson, H.G. (1977), 'Comment on D. Currie: Some Criticisms of the Monetary Analysis of Balance of Payments Correction', *Economic Journal*, 87, pp. 769–70.

North, D. (1691), *Discourses upon Trade*, London.

Oates, W.E. (1966), 'Budget Balance and Equilibrium Income: A Comment on the Efficacy of Fiscal and Monetary Policy in an Open Economy', *Journal of Finance*, 21, pp. 489–98.

Obstfeld, M. (1982), 'Can We Sterilize? Theory and Evidence', *American Economic Association Papers and Proceedings*, May, pp. 45–55.

Ohlin, B. (1928), 'The Reparations Problem', *Index*.

Oppenheimer, P.M. (1974), 'Non-Traded Goods and the Balance of Payments: A Historical Note', *Journal of Economic Literature*, 12, pp. 882–8.

Ott, D.J. and Ott, A.F. (1965), 'Budget Balance and Equilibrium Income', *Journal of Finance*, 20, pp. 71–7.

Pagan, A.R. and Tanaka, K. (1979), *A Further Test for Assessing the Stability of Regression Coefficients*, mimeo, Australian National University.

Page, E.S. (1954), 'Continuous Inspection Schemes', *Biometrika*, 41, pp. 100–14.

Paish, F.W. (1936), 'Banking Policy and the Balance of International Payments', *Economica*, 3, pp. 404–22.

Patrick, H. and Rosovsky, H. (eds) (1976), *Asia's New Giant*, Washington, D.C.: Brookings Institution.

Pearce, I.F. (1961), 'The Problem of the Balance of Payments', *International Economic Review*, 2, pp. 1–28.

Petty, W. (1662), *A Treatise of Taxes and Contributions*, London.

Pigou, A.C. (1932), 'The Effect of Reparations on the Ratio of International Exchange', *Economic Journal*, 42, pp. 532–43.

Plackett, R.L. (1950), 'Some Theorems in Least Squares', *Biometrika*, 41, pp. 100–14.

Polak, J.J. (1957), 'Monetary Analysis of Income Formation and Payments Problems', *International Monetary Fund Staff Papers*, 6, pp. 1–50.

Putnam, B.H. and Wilford, D.S. (1977), *International Reserve Flows: Seemingly Unrelated Regressions*, mimeo, International Monetary Fund, Washington, D.C.

Quandt, R.E. (1958), 'The Estimation of the Parameters of a Linear Regression System Obeying Two Separate Regimes', *Journal of the American Statistical Association*, 53, pp. 873–80.

Quandt, R.E. (1960), 'Tests of the Hypothesis that a Linear Regression System Obeys Two Separate Regimes', *Journal of the American Statistical Association*, 60, pp. 324–30.

Raj, B. and Ullah, A. (1981), *Econometrics: A Varying Coefficients Approach*, London: Croom Helm.

Rao, C.R. (1965), 'The Theory of Least Squares when the Parameters are Stochastic and its Application to the Analysis of Growth Curves', *Biometrika*, 52, pp. 447–58.

Rao, C.R. (1973), *Linear Statistical Inference and its Applications*, New York: Wiley.

Rao, P. (1974), 'Specification Bias in Seemingly Unrelated Regressions', in Sellekaerts, W. (ed.), *Essays in Honor of Tinbergen*, vol. 2, New York: International Arts and Sciences Press.

Rhomberg, R.R. and Heller, R.H. (1977), 'Introductory Survey', in *The Monetary Approach to the Balance of Payments*, International Monetary Fund, Washington, D.C.

Ricardo, D. (1810), *The High Price of Bullion: A Proof of the Depreciation of Bank Notes*, London.

Ricardo, D. (1821), *On the Principles of Political Economy and Taxation*, London.

Robinson, J. (1937), 'The Foreign Exchanges', in her *Essays in the Theory of Employment*, Cambridge.

Rosenberg, B. (1968), *Varying Parameter Estimation*, doctoral thesis, Harvard University.

Rosenberg, B. (1973), 'The Analysis of a Cross Section of Time Series by Stochastically Convergent Parameter Regression', *Annals of Economic and Social Measurement*, 2, pp. 399–428.

Rubin, H. (1950), 'Note on Random Coefficients', in Koopmans, T.C. (ed.), *Statistical Inference in Dynamic Models*, Cowles Commission Monograph No. 10, New Haven, Conn.: Yale University Press.

Salter, W.E.G. (1959), 'Internal and External Balance: The Role of Price and Expenditure Effects', *Economic Record*, 35, pp. 226–38.

Sargan, J.D. (1958), 'The Estimation of Economic Relationships using Instrumental Variables', *Econometrica*, 26, pp. 393–413.

Sarris, A.H. (1973), 'A Bayesian Approach to Estimation of Time-Varying Regression Coefficients', *Annals of Economic and Social Measurement*, 4 (special issue on time-varying parameters), pp. 501–23.

Schultz, H. (1937), *The Theory and Measurement of Demand*, Chicago: Chicago University Press.

Schumpeter, J.A. (1954), *History of Economic Analysis*, London: George Allen and Unwin.

Schweppe, F.C. (1965), 'Evaluation of Likelihood Functions for Gaussian Signals', *IEEE Transactions on Information Theory*, 11, pp. 61–70.

Schwert, G.W. (1979), 'Tests of Causality: The Message in the Innovations', *Journal of Monetary Economics*, Carnegie–Rochester Conference Supplement, 10, pp. 55–96.

Seligman, E.R.A. (1930), 'Bullionists', in Seligman, E.R.A. (ed.), *Encyclopaedia of the Social Sciences*, New York: Macmillan.

Senior, N. (1830), *Three Lectures on the Cost of Obtaining Money*, Oxford.

Silvey, S.D. (1970), *Statistical Inference*, London: Penguin.

Sims, C.A. (1972), 'Money, Income and Causality', *American Economic Review*, 62, pp. 540–52.

Skoog, G.R. (1976), *Causality Characterizations: Bivariate, Trivariate, and Multivariate Propositions*, Federal Reserve Bank of Minneapolis.

Slough, J.R. (1981), *Granger–Sims Causality: A Brief Survey of its Use and Misuse*, mimeo, National Science Foundation.

Smith, A. (1759), *The Theory of Moral Sentiments*, London. (References to edition of E. Cannan, 1904, Oxford.)

Smith, A. (1776), *An Inquiry into the Nature and Causes of the Wealth of Nations*, London. (References to edition of E. Cannan, 1904, Oxford.)

Smith, A. (1896), *Lectures on Justice, Police, Revenue and Arms, Delivered in the University of Glasgow by Adam Smith, Reported by a Student in 1763*, (ed. E. Cannan), Oxford.

Sohmen, E. (1957), 'Demand Elasticities and the Foreign Exchange Market', *Journal of Political Economy*, 65, pp. 431–6.

Spreen, T.H. and Shankwiler, J.S. (1979), 'Causal Relationships in the Fed Cattle Market', *Southern Journal of Agricultural Economics*, 13, pp. 149–53.

Steigum, E.J. (1980), *Keynesian and Classical Unemployment in an Open Economy*, mimeo, Norwegian School of Economics, Bergen, Norway.

Swan, T.W. (1963), 'Longer-Run Problems of the Balance of Payments', in Arndt, H.W. and Corden, M. (eds), *The Australian Economy*, Melbourne: Chesire.

Swoboda, A.K. (1973), 'Monetary Policy under Fixed Exchange Rates: Effectiveness, the Speed of Adjustment, and Proper Use', *Economica*, 41, pp. 136–54.

Swoboda, A.K. (1977), 'Monetary Approaches to Worldwide Inflation', in Krause, L.B. and Salant, W. (eds), *Worldwide Inflation: Theory and Recent Experience*, Washington: Brookings Institution.

Swoboda, A.K. and Dornbusch, R. (1973), 'Adjustment, Policy and Monetary Equilibrium in a Two-Country Model', in Connolly, M. and Swoboda, A.K. (eds), *International Trade and Money*, London: George Allen and Unwin.

Takayama, A. (1969), 'The Effects of Fiscal and Monetary Policies under Flexible and Fixed Exchange Rates', *Canadian Journal of Economics*, 2, pp. 190–209.

Taussig, F.W. (1928), *International Trade*, New York: Macmillan.

Taylor, M.P. (1987), 'On Granger Causality and the Monetary Approach to the Balance of Payments', *Journal of Macroeconomics*, 9, pp. 239–54.

Tew, B. (1970), *International Monetary Cooperation, 1945–70*, London: Hutchinson.

Theil, H. (1971), *Principles of Econometrics*, Amsterdam: North Holland.

Theil, H. and Mennes, L.B.M. (1959), *Multiplicative Randomness in Time Series Regression Analysis*, Report 5901, Econometric Institute of the Netherlands School of Economics, Rotterdam.

Theil, M. and Goldberger, A.S. (1961), 'On Pure and Mixed Statistical Estimation in Economics', *International Economic Review*, 2, pp. 65–78.

Thornton, H. (1802), *Paper Credit of Great Britain*, London.

Tinbergen, J. (1952), *On the Theory of Economic Policy*, Amsterdam: North Holland.

Tobin, J.E. (1965), 'The Theory of Portfolio Selection', in Hahn, F.H. and Brechling, F.P.R. (eds), *The Theory of Interest Rates: Proceedings of a Conference Held by the International Economic Association*, London.

Tobin, J. (1969), 'A General Equilibrium Approach to Monetary Theory', *Journal of Money, Credit and Banking*, 1, pp. 15–29.

Tsiang, S.C. (1961), 'The Role of Money in Trade-Balance Stability: Synthesis of the Elasticity and Absorption Approaches', *American Economic Review*, 51, pp. 912–36.

Ujiie, J. (1978), 'A Stock Adjustment Approach to Monetary Policy and the Balance of Payments', in Frenkel and Johnson (1978).

Venderlint, J. (1734), *Money Answers All Things*, London.

Viner, J. (1924), *Canada's Balance of International Indebtedness, 1900-1913*, Cambridge, Mass.: Harvard University Press.

Viner, J. (1937), *Studies in the Theory of International Trade*, New York: Harper.

Viner, J. (1968), 'Economic Thought: Mercantilist Thought', in Sills, D.L. (ed.), *International Encyclopaedia of the Social Sciences*, New York: Macmillan.

Wald, A. (1947), 'A Note on Regression Analysis', *Annals of Mathematical Statistics*, 18, pp. 586-9.

Wallis, K.F. (1972), 'Testing for Fourth-Order Serial Correlation in Quarterly Regression Models', *Econometrica*, 40, pp. 617-36.

Waugh, F.V. (1943), 'Choice of the Dependent Variable in Regression Analysis', *Journal of the American Statistical Association*, March, pp. 210-13.

Wheatley, J. (1807), *An Essay on the Theory of Money*, London.

White, H. (1980), 'A Heteroskedasticity Consistent Covariance Matrix Estimator and a Direct Test for Heteroskedasticity', *Econometrica*, 48, pp. 817-38.

White, H.D. (1933), *The French International Accounts, 1880-1913*, Cambridge, Mass.

Whitman, M.v.N. (1974), 'The Current and Future Role of the Dollar: How Much Symmetry?', *Brookings Papers on Economic Activity*, 1974(3), pp. 539-83.

Whitman, M.v.N. (1975), 'Global Monetarism and the Monetary Approach to the Balance of Payments', *Brookings Papers on Economic Activity*, 1975(3), pp. 491-536.

Wiener, N. (1956), 'The Theory of Prediction', in Beckenback, E.F. (ed.), *Modern Mathematics for Engineers*, New York: McGraw-Hill.

Willett, T.D. (1967), *A Portfolio Theory of International Short-Term Capital Movements: With A Critique of Recent United States Empirical Studies*, doctoral thesis, University of Virginia.

Willett, T.D. and Forte, F. (1969), 'Interest Rate Policy and External Balance', *Quarterly Journal of Economics*, 83, pp. 242–62.

Williams, D., Goodhart, C.A.E. and Gowland, D.H. (1976), 'Money, Income and Causality: The UK Experience', *American Economic Review*, 66, pp. 417–23.

Williams, J.H. (1920), *Argentine International Trade Under Inconvertible Paper Money, 1880–1900*, Cambridge, Mass.

Williamson, J. (1977), *The Failure of World Monetary Reform, 1971–74*, London: Nelson.

Wold, H. (1953), *Demand Analysis — A Study in Econometrics*, New York: Wiley.

Woodward, R.H. and Goldsmith, P.L. (1964), *Cumulative Sum Techniques*, Monograph No. 3, ICI Series on Mathematical and Statistical Techniques for Industry, Edinburgh: Oliver and Boyd.

Wu, D. (1973), 'Alternative Tests of Independence between Stochastic Regressors and Disturbances', *Econometrica*, 41, pp. 733–50.

Zecher, J.R. (1976), 'Monetary Equilibrium and International Reserve Flows in Australia', in Frenkel and Johnson (1976).

Zellner, A. (1962), 'An Efficient Method of Estimating Seemingly Unrelated Regressions and Tests of Aggregation Bias', *Journal of the American Statistical Association*, 57, pp. 348–68.

Zellner, A. (1966), *On the Aggregation Problem: A New Approach to a Troublesome Problem*, Report No. 6628, Center of Mathematical Studies in Business and Economics, University of Chicago.

Zellner, A. (1979), 'Causality and Econometrics', *Journal of Monetary Economics*, Carnegie–Rochester Conference Supplement, 10, pp. 9–54.

Author Index

Subject Index

Printed in Great Britain by
Billing & Sons Ltd, Worcester